CALCULA

THE DATES OF THE BIRTH
AND CRUCIFIXION OF
JESUS

CALCULATING
THE DATES OF THE BIRTH
AND CRUCIFIXION OF
JESUS

James A. Nollet

REDEMPTION
PRESS

Published by Redemption Press, PO Box 427, Enumclaw, WA 98022
Toll Free (844) 2REDEEM (273-3336)

Redemption Press is honored to present this title in partnership with the author. The views expressed or implied in this work are those of the author. Redemption Press provides our imprint seal representing design excellence, creative content and high quality production.

The image of the full moon under partial eclipse on the evening of April 3, AD 33, at the point of moonrise in Jerusalem, found on the back cover, was generated with the Starry Night Enthusiast 7 astronomy program. Starry Nights Enthusiast 7, © 2009, is a publication of The Simulation Corporation; 111 Jarvis Street, 2nd Floor; Toronto, ON; M5C 2H4 Canada.

Scripture verses taken from the New Testament are from the King James Version of the Bible.

Scripture verses taken from the Old Testament, unless otherwise noted, are from *The Pentateuch and Rashi's Commentary,* by the Rabbis Abraham ben Isaiah and Benjamin Sharpman, in collaboration with Dr. Harry M. Orlinsky and Rabbi Dr. Morris Charner (Philadelphia: S.S. & R Publishing Company, Inc., 1949, the press of the Jewish Publication Society.

ISBN 13: 978-1-63232-608-9 (Print)
          978-1-63232-609-6 (ePub)
          978-1-63232-611-9 (Mobi)

Library of Congress Catalog Card Number: 2015946011

CONTENTS

ACKNOWLEDGMENTS

I gratefully acknowledge the kindly and fatherly attentions rendered unto me by the professors Sir Dr. Colin J. Humphreys and Dr. John P. Pratt. I would not have published this book had it not been for the advice and encouragement of these two scholars, particularly that of Dr. Humphreys.

FOREWORD

J esus of Nazareth died on April 3, AD 33. That is the sum and distilled substance of this book. If having my (presumably) informed opinion on that fact is all you want or need, you need read no further. However, since you, the reader, paid good money to buy this book, I hope and trust you will read further, study, and ponder this book. I'm confident that the effort involved will reward you by strengthening the level of your overall knowledge, and whatever belief and faith in Jesus Christ you brought to this book.[1]

I want to say a short preliminary word about what this book is, and is not, and how it came into this present form.

This book is neither astrology nor numerology. It uses no arcane counting of Bible verses or "weeks of Daniel" or such methods to arrive at its conclusion. The method of this book is implied from its very title—scientific. It combines texts of the New Testament primarily, together with certain texts from the Old Testament, and examines these in the light of a) known historical facts, b) Judaism, and c) good old-fashioned astronomy.

This book asks the reader to accept little or nothing on blind faith. Rather, it is intended to present the reader with known *facts* that are generally agreed upon, or at least can be defended rationally, and to follow a chain of reasoning which can be understood logically and rationally.

This book will also assume, wherever possible, that the Gospels are accurate, though we will see that the Gospels themselves disagree as to whether the events of the Last Supper happened on the day of Passover itself, or on the day before.

Here is how this work came about: In the 1980s my mother wrote Regency romance novels for Harlequin and other such publishers. In the course of researching one of her stories, she needed to know when Pentecost occurred in a particular year shortly after the conclusion of the Napoleonic wars. My father rang me and asked me if this could be ascertained.

Now it would be easy, since perpetual Jewish and Christian calendars are readily available online, but even as recently as the 1980s, such information was hard to come by, at least without going to the trouble of visiting a good library. However, I knew how the Jewish and Christian perpetual calendars worked (both are ultimately lunar-based), *and* I had a very primitive computer—a Commodore '64—with a similarly primitive and slow astronomy program, and with these two, I was readily able to come up with the correct date.

This got me to thinking—would it be possible to calculate a correct date for the Crucifixion as well? So I went to work—and found it *was* possible.

Time went on, and I found an urge to present my findings into a booklet that I could then market and sell myself. By that time, I had a much better computer with Windows 95, and a similarly better astronomy program. So I went to work and *did no research whatsoever*, other than from sacred texts themselves, my own personal knowledge, my personal library, and my astronomy program, and published my findings in a booklet called *A Scientific Determination: the Exact Time and Date of the Death of Jesus of*

Nazareth. I worked this way because I didn't want someone else's work to influence or bias my own work.

I self-published and attempted to market my booklet, with *some* degree of success— though I still have a hundred or so extra copies left unsold/undistributed, which I'm looking at as I type these very words!

After everything was done, *then* I checked the Internet, and found to my frank dismay—*uh-oh*—someone had already beaten me to the punch. Sixteen years previously, in 1983, two English scientists by the names of Drs. Humphreys and Waddington had their paper on the same subject published in *Nature* magazine. While I was quite happy that my own findings independently agreed with the findings of these two eminent, full-time scientists, still, I found to my chagrin that I'd been scooped.

Or—had I really been scooped? In some particulars, indeed, in *the most important* particular, yes. However, my method and reasoning differed sharply in some respects from that of the two esteemed Englishmen, so I thought I still had a basis for believing that I'd written an original work.

Such did matters rest until 2011, when it came to my attention that a certain someone I'll not name had self-published his own novel on Kindle. Though I dislike this person, his energy and industry were nevertheless eye-opening. I reasoned to myself, if *he* could self-publish, then *anyone* can, so I therefore began thinking maybe I should reissue my old booklet.

Before I would do such a thing, I first wanted to try to contact Sir Dr. Colin J. Humphreys himself if I could, present him with my booklet, and get his opinion as to whether I should attempt to self-publish it. I tracked him down at his office as the chair of the Metallurgy Department of Cambridge University, UK. He in turn very graciously, and *gratis*, too!, sent me a signed copy of his own recent book on the subject of dating the Crucifixion. His book is titled *The Mystery of the Last Supper*, and actually breaks some new ground beyond that which he covered in his 1983 paper. His book re-proves his own finding about the correct date of the Crucifixion, but goes much beyond that too, in that it also reconciles and harmonizes certain difficulties and apparent errors and contradictions that arise in the various Gospel accounts of the Crucifixion. It's a brilliant work, published by the Cambridge University Press, and I recommend it heartily to anyone who is interested in the subject!

Much of Dr. Humphreys' book is a defense of his theory that says Jesus followed an old-style Jewish calendar which stopped being used by the Jews on account of the Babylonian captivity, in which days began at sun*rise*, not sunset, and in which months commenced on the first *morning* after the *final* sighting of the *old* moon, and not on the first *evening* of the sighting of the *new* moon, the latter of which have been the prevailing custom of the Jewish people for many centuries.

Basically, Dr. Humphreys claims that Jesus was using an old-style calendrical system, which actually was common in Galilee where he came from, but which the rest of the Jews farther south were not using, in which his months commenced a day or more before the rest of the Jewish world.

His theory accounts for why Jesus, in the Synoptic Gospels, celebrated Passover on *Thursday* night in the year of his Crucifixion, even though I can prove below that this was *impossible* (in a new moon-based calendar) since, in none of the possible years of the Crucifixion did Passover ever fall on a Thursday night. Also the Gospel of John confirms that the events of the Last Supper through the Crucifixion all happened on the day *before* Passover.

Yes indeed, Jerusalem *never* observed Passover on Thursday night in any year in which Jesus might have been crucified. But that does *not* mean that Jesus *himself* didn't observe the Passover on that Thursday night.

It is with this theory of an alternate, pre-exilic calendar that Dr. Humphreys can reconcile the apparent problems and disagreements that appear in the Gospels' account of the week of the Crucifixion.

This book need not, and will not concern itself with the issue of which calendar Jesus may have used. As Dr. Humphreys himself would agree, it is eminently possible to prove the date of the Crucifixion without regard to which version of the Jewish calendar Jesus may have used.

When I received Dr. Humphreys' book, initially, I groaned, for I said to myself, *now I really shouldn't reissue my book*. But I pored through his book and sent him back an eighty-page critique, which he evidently found most valuable and even at times astonishing. Mostly, my comments complemented his book since, for the most part, I agreed with him, though I didn't hesitate to tell him when I did not.

This, however, still left open the question, should I self-publish this book? On the one hand, I do have numerous and unique ways of looking at the subject of dating the Crucifixion that have never appeared before, not even in Dr. Humphreys works, and which should be known, disseminated, and discussed. But on the other hand, Dr. Humphreys has already done an excellent job of proving the date of the Crucifixion, so my work could therefore, arguably, be considered redundant.

Dr. Humphreys himself has made his recommendation, and it is one I will follow. Here are his own words to me: " . . . I want to say that your booklet is excellent, with many important insights. I do encourage you to publish it. It is wonderfully written."[2]

Well! With such a wonderful recommendation, who am I to demur? So with that, I now present the following case for the determination of the precise date of the Crucifixion of Jesus of Nazareth.

CHAPTER 1

IN WHAT YEAR DID JESUS DIE?

Too many years ago when I was but a tad of a lad and attended Catholic parochial schools, the nuns taught us that Jesus was born "in the year 0,"[1] lived thirty years in quiet anonymity,[2] and then had a public career which lasted for three years and culminated in his Crucifixion, Resurrection, and subsequent Ascension, and it all therefore happened in the year 33.[3]

But the Gospels don't record the year of his death. And tradition often has dubious reliability. For example, the traditional contention that Jesus was born in the year 1 BC or AD is a contention that many people have disputed (more about that in the following chapter about fixing the date of the Nativity).

It is not the primary purpose of this book to find the date of Jesus' birth, which in any event is impossible to pinpoint precisely, simply because there is not enough information.

However, the date of Jesus' birth *may* have *some* bearing on finding the year when he died, in light of Luke's remark (indicated below in Note 3) that Jesus was "about thirty years old" when he began his ministry. So before we try to calculate when Jesus died, the following chapter will, as briefly as possible, touch upon the arguments for dating Jesus' birth.

CHAPTER 2

WHAT CAN WE SAY ABOUT WHEN JESUS WAS BORN?

Nota Bene: A condensed version of this chapter has already been published, in a peer-reviewed article, "Astronomical and Historical Evidence for Dating the Nativity in 2 BC," in Vol. 64, No. 4 of *Perspectives on Science and Christian Faith*. This article is available for public viewing from their website, www. asa3.org.

There are actually many estimates for the year of the birth of Jesus.

A. T. Olmstead thought it was as early as 20 BC.[1]

E. Jerry Vardaman thought Jesus was born as early as 12 BC.[2]

C. Ogg thought the birth happened in 11 BC.[3]

In AD 180, the Christian writer Iraeneus placed the birth of Jesus in the forty-fourth year of the reign of the Emperor Augustus, about 3/2 BC.[4]

In AD 194, Clement of Alexandria estimated that Jesus was born 194 years before the death of the Emperor Commodus (who eventually achieved villainous movie fame in *The Rise and Fall of the Roman Empire*, with Stephen Boyd and Sophia Loren, and later in *Gladiator* with Russell Crowe). Commodus died on the last day of AD 192; therefore Jesus was born around 2 BC.[5]

In AD 198, Tertullian said that Jesus was born twenty-eight years after the deaths of Marcus Antonius and Queen Cleopatra, and that he was born fifteen years before the death of Caesar Augustus.[6] Antony & Cleopatra died in the year following the Battle of Actium (31 BC), so this would place the year of Jesus' birth as 2 BC. On the other hand, Augustus died in AD 14, so this would place the birth of Jesus in 1 BC. Origen,[7] writing a few decades later, also said that Augustus lived for fifteen years after the birth of Jesus, also placing that in the year 1 BC. He also correctly noted that Augustus reigned for fifty-six years (44 BC–AD 14) following the assassination of Julius Caesar, but said that Jesus was born in the forty-first year of Augustus' reign, which would place it in 3 BC.

There were attempts in ancient times to estimate the number of years from Adam to the birth of Jesus. Demetrius and Eupolemus said that there were 5307 years before the birth of Jesus, and called this calendar A.Ad, or *Anno Adami*. This calendar is also called AM, or *Anno Mundi*, literally "the year of the world." It was the system used during the age of the Byzantine Empire. Julius Africanus also used this system, but said there were 5500 years A.Ad. from Adam to the birth of Jesus, which would correspond to what we call 3/2 BC. Hippolytus of Rome concurred, but said that Jesus was born in 5502 A.Ad. Both of these writers lived in the early third century.

(These systems are at large variance with the traditional Jewish calculations for dating the passing years. According to Judaism, 3760 years passed "BCE"—"Before the Common Era"—before the Year 1 CE ["Common Era"], when our present era commenced. The Year 1 CE = the Year AD 1 = the year 3761 from the creation of the world.)

Early in the fourth century, Eusebius wrote[8] that Jesus was born in the forty-second year of the reign of Augustus, and in the twenty-eight year after the death of Cleopatra. Leaving aside the issue of whether Eusebius intended to count inclusively or exclusively, that places the birth of Jesus at around 2 BC.

In the middle of the fourth century, Epiphanius[9] agreed. On the other hand, Epiphanius also notes the opinion of the "Alogi," a group of heretics who opposed the Gospel of John (hence the name "A-logi," since *logos* is a critical word in the opening of John's Gospel). On the one hand, they held the birth of Jesus occurred in 4 BC; but on the other hand, they also held it occurred during the consulships of S. Camerinus and B. Pompeianus (Poppaeus Sabinus), who were consuls in AD 9 AD.

In 418, Paulus Orosius[10] wrote that Jesus was born in 752 AUC, which is 2 BC.

Senator Cassiodorus, writing after the final fall of the Western Roman Empire (476, when there were no more senators), wrote that Jesus was born in the forty-first year of the reign of Augustus, when C. Lentulus and M. Messala were consuls, both of which happened in 3 BC.

Dionysios Exiguus, as already noted, also writing in the sixth century, said Jesus was born specifically on December 25, 1 BC, which of course was one week before the era of BC yielded to AD.

And finally, in modern times, Bishop Ussher (of Armagh, in Ireland) in the seventeenth century proposed that the world was created precisely on October 22, 4004 BC. Since Ussher proposed this after Pope Gregory XIII instituted the Gregorian Reform (which we use to this day) of the old calendar of Julius Caesar, I don't know if this date includes or not the ten days which Pope Gregory cancelled (by papal decree, October 5-14, 1582 never existed; this is something we will discuss in greater depth later on). By the way, Ussher's Creation in October roughly agrees, with the opinion of Judaism, which holds that Rosh HaShanah, which occurs about in mid-to-late September, marks the anniversary of Creation. Anyway, Bishop Ussher said Jesus was born flatly in the year 4000 AM, which corresponds to 4 BC.

Such are the beliefs of scholars throughout history.

Currently, many scholars and believers say that Jesus was born around 4 BC or possibly earlier, because in Matthew's Nativity narrative, King Herod was alive for up to the first two years of Jesus' life, and it's generally believed he died in 4 BC. In the Gospel account, King Herod slew all the male babies of Bethlehem who were two years of age and under. So if he died in 4 BC, and tried to kill a baby whom he supposed could have been two years old, that might place the year of Jesus' birth in 6 BC.

On the other hand, the Gospel of Luke states that there was a universal census of the Roman world shortly before Jesus was born, when P. Sulpicius Quirinius was governor of Syria. Quirinius was governor twice, in 3 BC[11] and in AD 6. However, we generally and popularly suppose that Luke clearly must be referring to the latter term, because that was a year a local census for taxation purposes occurred.

According to Flavius Josephus,[12] the Emperor Augustus sent Quirinius to be governor of Syria at the same time he sent Coponius to be the first procurator of Judea. This was necessary because prior to AD 6, Judea had been ruled by Herod Archelaus, who was one of King Herod's surviving sons, and who took over after Herod died. The Romans deposed him in AD 6 and annexed Judea directly to the empire. This was the reason for the census. Prior to deposing Herod Archelaus, the Romans had been content to extract an annual tribute from him, and didn't care how many people lived there. After they seized direct control, they needed to count noses so they'd have a better idea how much in taxes they could reasonably demand from Judea.

Josephus further states[13] that this census occurred in the thirty-seventh year "after Caesar's victory over Antony at Actium" (31 BC), which, counting inclusively, brings us to AD 6. (The reader should make note of this manner of dating from the year of the Battle of Actium because, believe it or not, it will play a small role later on in determining the date of the Crucifixion.)

It can be briefly here noted that Tertullian[14] believed that Luke's census took place while C. Sentius Saturninus was governor of Syria (4–2 BC).[15] In the *Res Gestae Divi Augusti*, Augustus himself noted that the senate awarded him the title of *Pater Patriae* (Father of the Country) in his thirteenth consulship, which was 2 BC. This honorific may have required all persons to register and take an oath affirming Augustus in this title. Josephus[16] noted that all the Jews of Judea were required to take this oath, but 6,000 Pharisees refused. Orosius[17] certainly believed that this honorific required a universal registration and census, and believed this was the census to which Luke referred. Quirinius was indeed governor of Syria at this time also, but Coponius wouldn't become procurator of Judea for another eight to nine, so Josephus' account seems to knock this down.

It is this book's intention to regard the words of the Gospel as stipulated fact unless circumstances compel otherwise. I regard it as possible that Flavius Josephus got his fact wrong about Coponius, thereby confusing Quirinius' first term as governor with his second term. If so, and if we also note and disregard the evident error which Tertullian made[15] by misidentifying which census of Augustus involved the birth of Jesus, most of the discrepancy between the dates of the Nativity which existed between Luke and Matthew vanish, thereby placing Luke's census and subsequent nativity, not in AD 6, but 2 BC. As we will see, we *might* be able to make *all* of the apparent discrepancy between Luke and Matthew vanish!

That most modern opinion places the death of King Herod in 4 BC is indisputable.

I have before me as I write these words a certain book that I inherited from my beloved grandfather Dowsley Clark. It is *An Encyclopedia of WORLD HISTORY*, originally published in 1940 by the Houghton-Mifflin Company of Boston. It says, "Jesus of Nazareth was born in the latter part of (King Herod's) reign, between 6 and 4 BC."[18]

Pope Benedict XVI, of all people, very recently weighed in on this precise issue. One should note that until recently he was the head of the Catholic Church, an organization that is steeped in tradition. Its tradition says that Jesus was born in 1 BC (or even "0 BC"), so for the pope to break with this, or any tradition publicly, is a remarkable thing. But Pope Benedict is also a scholar of the first water who only welcomes the opportunity to meld old traditions with modern knowledge.

He recently wrote and published a three-volume biography of Jesus. His most recent installment was *The Infancy Narratives*, and I quote from it:

> One initial problem can be solved quite easily: the census took place at the time of King Herod the Great, who actually died in the year 4 BC. The starting-point for our reckoning of time—the calculation of Jesus' date of birth—goes back to the monk Dionysius Exiguus (died c. 550) who evidently miscalculated by a few years. The historical date of the birth of Jesus is therefore to be placed a few years earlier."[19]

Traditional Argument Placing Jesus' Birth from 6–4 BC

John P. Pratt summarizes the argument very well and succinctly for placing the birth of Jesus from 6–4 BC, so I will simply quote from his paper.[20]

Josephus says that Varus was Governor of Syria at Herod's death and Varus is indeed indicated as such in 4 BC by coins.[21] The problem, pointed out by Martin,[22] is that the coins also show Varus was Governor in 6 and 5 BC, whereas Josephus indicates that Saturninus was Governor for the two years preceding Herod's death.[23] Martin's solution is that an inscription found near Varus' villa, which describes a man who was twice Governor of Syria, probably refers to Varus [See Note 15]. If so, his second term could well have been about 1 BC, when there is no record of anyone else as Governor.

Pratt goes on to say:

The principal source for the life of Herod is the works of (Flavius) Josephus,[24] a Jewish historian who wrote near the end of the first century. His methods are not always clear and he is sometimes inconsistent so care must be exercised to cross-check his chronology with other sources. Events that are also dated in Roman history are usually the strongest evidence to correlate his history with our calendar. Josephus states that Herod captured Jerusalem and began to reign in what we would call 37 BC, and lived for 34 years thereafter, implying his death was in 4 – 3 BC. Other evidence both from Josephus and coins indicates that his successors began to reign in 4 - 3 BC. Moreover, Josephus also mentions a lunar eclipse shortly before Herod's death.[25] For centuries the evidence from astronomy has appeared decisive; a lunar eclipse occurred on March 13, 4 BC, whereas there was no such eclipse visible in Palestine in 3 BC. Thus, the eclipse has played a crucial role in the traditional conclusion that Herod died in the spring of 4 BC (and Jesus was therefore born as early as 6 BC).

In short: The *sole* basis for the belief that Jesus was born from 6 BC–4 BC depends on Flavius Josephus, his account of the death of King Herod, and the eclipse he reported. But how r*eliable* is this?

Some scholars have noted that this eclipse is unsuitable, because a) it happened only one month before that year's Passover, between which time b) Herod became sick and died of a horrible wasting disease; but not before c) he was taken to warm baths and treated; d) executed his son Herod Antipater after also having made him co-regent (causing a bemused Caesar Augustus to observe that it was better to be Herod's pig than his son, since Jews don't kill or eat pigs); e) died and was buried after a magnificent funeral which needed at least days to prepare; f) followed by a seven-day mourning period; g) followed by yet another mourning period for those whom Herod had executed before the eclipse. These scholars believe one month isn't nearly enough time to account for all these events, so they've browsed around for other eclipses that give a more generous and realistic span of time for these events to unfold.

Barnes[26] preferred the eclipse of September 15, 5 BC for this very reason; six months is enough time for all the above events to occur. However, Martin[27] disagreed, arguing that this would mean that Herod Archelaus would have waited six months, until after the following Passover, before going to Rome and asking Caesar Augustus to confirm him as the next king. Furthermore, if Herod died sometime in 5 BC, that could mean Jesus conceivably was born in 7 BC, which is simply too early.

Flavius Josephus actually dated the length of Herod's kingship in *two* different ways. The first way is that Josephus says Herod received his kingship from two of the three Triumvirs Marcus Antonius (Antony) and Gaius Octavius (the future Caesar Augustus) in the year Gnaeus Domitius Calvinus (for the second time) and Gaius Asinius Pollio were consuls, which was 40 BC,[28] and from this date counts thirty-seven years to Herod's death.

The second way is that Josephus says Herod captured Jerusalem and killed his chief rival in the year when Marcus Agrippa and Caninius Gallus were consuls (37 BC), and thereafter ruled for thirty-four years. However, in this case, and since Jewish regnal years commenced on 1 Nisan,[29] that would mean that King Herod's year 1 began around the time of the vernal equinox in the spring of 36. If King Herod died in the thirty-fourth year of his reign thereafter, he'd have died in 3 BC or even 2 BC.

In fact, if King Herod died shortly before Passover, then according to Josephus' thirty-four-year countdown from the time of the taking of Jerusalem, King Herod *had* to have died early in 2 BC. Even if we count from 1 Nisan in the year 37 BC as year 1 of King Herod's rule, then King Herod *had* to have died early in the year 3 BC.

Furthermore, Josephus says that King Herod captured Jerusalem on *Yom Kippur,* the Day of Atonement, also the anniversary of the very day when the Roman Proconsul Gnaeus Pompeius Magnus (Pompey) likewise took Jerusalem *twenty-seven years earlier.*[28] Since Pompey did that in 63 BC, that would mean that King Herod actually captured Jerusalem, not in October 37 BC, but October 36 BC. If this is the case, we can then move the *earliest* possible date for the death of Herod to 1 BC, or maybe 2 BC at the *earliest.*

There was no eclipse of the moon visible in Judea either in 3 or 2 BC—more about *this* fact shortly.

With his 37/34-year regnal timelines, his eclipse, and his claim that Herod's surviving sons began their tetrarchies in 4 BC when he died, Flavius Josephus *seems* clearly to indicate that King Herod died in 4 BC–3 BC. But we now have seen that Josephus also contradicts this seemingly simple conclusion—which therefore leaves us with the conclusion that his 4 BC date simply can't be trusted—and therefore, too, the supposition that the eclipse of March 13, 4 BC heralded King Herod's forthcoming demise. As we can see, there are many inconsistencies with Josephus' account, as Dr. Pratt noted above.

Anyone wishing to follow Dr. Pratt's reasoning in full may do so by going to his website www.johnpratt.com. The essence of his argument is this: Before Herod executed his son Herod Antipater, he allowed Antipater to become co-regent with him.

This happened around 4 BC. After King Herod himself died, his surviving three sons, who became tetrarchs, all antedated their own reigns back to when Antipater was co-regent, in order to keep an unbroken chain between themselves and the deceased Antipater, thereby giving their own reigns more legitimacy. See more about this below.

So now the task is to find an eclipse of the moon that fits the facts of Herod's death as reported by Josephus. Before we do, let's look again at that eclipse of March 13, 4 BC, the eclipse which many scholars for a long time have regarded as the eclipse Josephus noted that preceded King Herod's death, even though we already now have solid evidence to suppose that King Herod actually died a few years later.

I have checked the *ephemeridae* of this eclipse with my astronomy program.[30] (I find no record of anybody else having done this, not even the Drs. Pratt, Humphreys, or Waddington.) This eclipse commenced at 12:07 A.M. local mean time[31] in Jerusalem on the night of March 12–3, 4 BC. In any lunar eclipse a "penumbral" period commences and concludes the eclipse, which means a part of the sun, but not all of the sun, is covered by the earth as its orbit places it between the sun and the moon. Because some sunlight is still striking the surface of the moon, this portion of the eclipse is either invisible or barely visible to the naked eye.

The umbral portion of the eclipse commenced almost exactly ninety minutes later, at 1:38 A.M. on the morning of March 13. The eclipse reached its maximum totality about an hour later, at 2:42 A.M., *but was only thirty-six percent total at the time of maximum totality.* The eclipse then receded for another two and a half-hours or so, concluding at around 5 A.M.

This is a *puny and minor* eclipse. Having seen a couple of dozen in my life, I know from experience that at this level of totality, the moon is still bright; it simply has a smudge in its corner. There is *no* reddening of the moon, characteristic of deep eclipses, at this minor level of totality.

It is a fact that in all of his writings, the eclipse that preceded Herod's death is the *sole and only* eclipse Josephus ever mentioned. But what a meek and puny little eclipse it was—if indeed *this* is the correct eclipse!

Furthermore, as Dr. Pratt notes in his paper, few if any souls in the ancient Jerusalem of 4 BC would even have been awake to behold this eclipse.

Given that this eclipse was insignificant, and moreover seen by next to nobody, it is *highly* unlikely that any memory of *this* eclipse survived for over seventy-five years by word-of-mouth, to be noted eventually by Flavius Josephus as shortly preceding the death of King Herod.

Given *all* of the problems associated with the March 13, 4 BC eclipse, Filmer[32] proposed the eclipse of January 10, 1 BC, as the eclipse associated by Josephus with the death of King Herod.

Given that this eclipse occurred at the full moon of the Jewish month of *Tevet*, a full three months before Passover, this solves all the chronological difficulties presented by the eclipse of March 13, 4 BC, giving ample time for all the events that occurred between the time of the eclipse and King Herod's death and its aftermath. Furthermore, unlike the puny eclipse of March 13, 4 BC, *this* eclipse must have been dramatic and grand, and worth reporting decades later to Flavius Josephus.

However, this eclipse too suffers from the same problem that plagued the eclipse of March 13, 4 BC—it simply happened way past everybody's bedtime.

Here are the *ephemeridae* for this eclipse:

First penumbral contact:	10:31 P.M. (January 9, 1 BC)
First umbral contact:	11:28 P.M.
Total eclipse:	12:25 A.M. (January 10)
Maximum totality:	1:15 A.M.
End of totality:	2:05 A.M.
Last umbral contact:	3:03 A.M.
Last penumbral contact; eclipse over:	4:00 A.M.

This eclipse would have begun to be palpably visible between 11:00–11:30 P.M. That's a couple of hours better than the 1:30 A.M. or so of the eclipse of March 13, 4 BC. But that benefit is halfway cancelled by the fact that the January 10 eclipse occurred at a time of the year when the sun went down (5:05 P.M.) a full fifty minutes earlier than it did on March 13, 4 BC (5:54 P.M.). This eclipse of January 10, 1 BC became palpably visible about six and a half hours after sundown, where the March 13, 4 BC eclipse became palpably visible about seven and three-quarter hours after sundown. In a time and place when people generally retired after darkness, there's little real difference between the remote timing of these eclipses; both would have been seen by few people.

And *especially* in January, when the nights even in Judea are a *lot* colder than they are in March, driving indoors even the riff-raff and denizens of the night. It's a safe bet that few people saw the eclipse of January 10, 1 BC. (I can personally attest to Jerusalem's climate, having spent most of January 1991 in Jerusalem, while Saddam Hussein was launching Scud missiles against Israel during the Gulf War.)

While we're at it, let's now look at the eclipse of September 15, 5 BC, which Barnes believed was the eclipse that Josephus said preceded the death of King Herod:

First penumbral contact: 7:46 P.M. (September 15, 5 BC)
First umbral contact: 8:44 P.M.
Total eclipse: 9:44 P.M.
Maximum totality: 10:34 P.M.
End of totality: 11:23 P.M.
Last umbral contact: 12:22 A.M. (September 16)
Last penumbral contact; eclipse over: 1:22 A.M.

This eclipse works better; it began to become palpably visible a couple of hours or so after sundown. But few people other than Barnes, for good reason, have ever believed this was the eclipse Flavius Josephus spoke about.

Finally, we arrive at the eclipse of December 29, 1 BC, which Dr. Pratt argues was the eclipse that preceded the death of King Herod.

Here are the *ephemeridae* of this eclipse:

First penumbral contact: 2:20 P.M. (December 29, 1 BC; note that this was during the day, before moon-rise, when the moon was still below the horizon, and invisible.)
First umbral contact: 3:28 P.M. (moon still invisible)
Maximum percentage of totality: 4:44 P.M. (moon still invisible; moon is under a 57 percent partial eclipse)
Time of complete moonrise: 5:02 P.M. (moon is 53 percent eclipsed)
Last umbral contact: 5:59 P.M.
Last penumbral contact; eclipse over: 7:07 P.M.

What to make of this eclipse?

Firstly, it was not a total eclipse, but only a partial eclipse. However, the moon was sufficiently covered to see the red color that is characteristic of most eclipses.

Furthermore, it is actually a highly *dramatic* thing to expect to see a normal full moon, but instead to see it rise misshapen and eclipsed. (I myself recently experienced this. On December 10, 2011, there was a total eclipse of the moon. I now live in Poland, and that evening after sundown, I was sitting at my desk looking eastward out my window. There were a lot of clouds that evening, and I saw the full moon rising as a crescent. At first, I thought a passing thick cloud was covering part of the moon, but when the dark area of the moon didn't change its shape, I realized that I was seeing a fading eclipse of the moon. It was momentarily startling.)

Dr. Pratt reasons that the dramatic nature of seeing a full moon rising under eclipse is a startling and dramatic thing that seldom happens, and which people tend to remember. Furthermore, the fact that it happened *at sunset* made it memorable because it meant that everybody was still awake and active and would have seen it—which is not the case with any of the other eclipses we've looked at.

(I myself still vividly remember another time, sometime in the late 1990s or so, when, living as I was in the USA in eastern Massachusetts at the time. On a fine, crisply cool, delicious evening that is characteristic of autumn and leaf-changing time in my beloved New England, the moon rose under a full, gorgeously ruby-red total eclipse. How *lovely* it was!)

Anyway, due to the dramatic nature of this eclipse, and due to the fact that many people must have witnessed it, for these reasons, Dr. Pratt believes the partial eclipse of December 29, 1 BC was the eclipse which Flavius Josephus says preceded and heralded the death of King Herod. (In fact, *both* of these eclipses occurred precisely three months before their respective Passovers.)

As does the eclipse of January of that year, this eclipse too gives enough time for the various events to happen that had to occur between the Josephus eclipse and the following Passover. If so, then King Herod died early in AD 1, and according to Dr. Pratt, Jesus was born sometime in 1 BC, perhaps around Passover.

How dramatic was this moonrise eclipse? Soon enough we will have occasion to consider what happened when a certain other full moon also rose under partial eclipse over Jerusalem. *This* eclipse was so dramatically timed that it altered the history of the world forever.

A couple of minor problems are left to resolve: Who was governor of Syria at the time of the census of the Nativity? And how well does this harmonize with Matthew's account of the infant Jesus being born before King Herod died? And what about Flavius Josephus mentioning that the sons of King Herod (other than the executed Antipater) came into their tetrarchies in 4 BC–3 BC, implying, as this does that King Herod died in 4 BC after all?

I now reproduce Tables 146 and 147 of Jack Finegan's *Handbook of Biblical Chronology*, both of which give listings of the governors or Syria from 9 BC–AD 7.

Year	Name of Governor Table 146	Name of Governor Table 147
9 BC	M. Titius	M. Titius
8 BC	C. Sentius Saturninus	M. Titius
7 BC	C. Sentius Saturninus	M. Titius, then P. Q. Varus
6 BC	Saturninus, then P. Q. Varus	P. Quinctilius Varus
5 BC	P. Quinctilius Varus	P. Quinctilius Varus
4 BC	P. Quinctilius Varus	Varus, then C. S. Saturninus
3 BC	P. Sulpicius Quirinius	C. Sentius Saturninus

Year	Name of Governor Table 146	Name of Governor Table 147
2 BC	P. Sulpicius Quirinius	Saturninus, then Varus
1 BC	Gaius Caesar	P. Quinctilius Varus
AD 1	Gaius Caesar	Varus, then Gaius Caesar
AD 2	Gaius Caesar	Gaius Caesar
AD 3	Gaius Caesar	Gaius Caesar
AD 4	G. Caesar, then L. V. Saturninus	Gaius Caesar
AD 5	L. Volusius Saturninus	
AD 6	P. Sulpicius Quirinius	
AD 7	P. Sulpicius Quirinius	

Gaius Caesar died[33] in Syria in AD 4 , so even if Table 147 doesn't mention his replacement, it's reasonable to suppose that L. Volusius Saturninus replaced him until AD 6 .

As Dr. Pratt noted, Josephus said that Varus was governor of Syria when Herod died. Looking at the above tables, we see general agreement that Varus began being governor in 6 BC and this continued into 4 BC. But then, in Table 147, there is a notation that Varus was *also* governor in 1 BC. Since this doesn't appear in Table 146, what does its appearance in 147 mean? Why is it there but not in the other table? And can we trust it?

The usually-accepted list of governors is from the Schürer-derived Table 146.[11] However, Tertullian's[34] comment that Sentius Saturninus was the governor when Augustus called his census has caused a scramble to revise the list of governors as reflected in Table 147 above.

The first question that arises is, Could Tertullian have confused this Saturninus with L. Volusius Saturninus, who according to Schürer (Table 146) was governor in AD 5, immediately preceding Quirinius? Given that Quirinius certainly followed this second Saturninus the following year (AD 6) and probably also was the governor in 3 BC and not the first Saturninus, the possibility of confusion certainly is present.

Tertullian, like Josephus, also gives us further reason to suspect his accuracy when he said, both that Jesus was born twenty-eight years after Antony and Cleopatra committed suicide (30 BC), which produces 2 BC, and that Jesus was born fifteen years before Augustus died in 14 AD, which makes Jesus born in 1 BC.

Neither Quirinius, nor either of the Saturnini, was governor in 1 BC. If C. Sentius Saturninus were governor in 2 BC, as Tertullian alleges, that means Quirinius was *not* governor. This contradicts Luke's Gospel that says Quirinius *was* the governor.

This is perhaps Tertullian's most unforgivable error, for he was a believing Christian, and lived at least a century after the Gospels were written and canonized into their present form. He *had* to have known about the Gospel of Luke that says that Quirinius was governor at the time of the census, but completely and callously ignored it, though doing so was almost tantamount to denial of the infallibility of Holy Scripture.

For this reason most of all, and on account of his other errors, we may therefore safely dismiss Tertullian's opinion that "Saturninus" was governor of Syria when Jesus was born.

So we are left with Varus as governor (whom Josephus said was governor when Herod died; therefore when Jesus was born), if Jesus were born in 4 BC, or with Quirinius if 3 BC or 2 BC.

But, what about Varus? We already noted (Notes 15 and 22) that a stone with an inscription was found near his old manor in 1784 referring to a certain unnamed man who was twice governor of Syria. Knowing that Varus was governor of Syria at least once, whom else could this refer to but Varus? But, if so, when so, if he stopped being governor in 4 BC?

If Quirinius were governor when Augustus called for the census—which meant that Herod was still alive—but Varus were governor when Herod died – that means Varus could *not* have followed Quirinius as governor after Quirinius stepped down after AD 7, because Herod was long dead even before AD 6. And, furthermore, after AD 7, Varus was involved with the legions in Germany (where the Germans wiped him and three legions out in AD 9).

The only way to make Luke and Josephus agree is to suppose that both Quirinius and Varus were twice governors. According to Schürer, Varus was governor in 4 BC and succeeded the following year by Quirinius (who therefore was governor of Syria for *both* of the *censi* which Augustus called for the Holy Land, one in 2 BC, to affirm him as *Pater Patriae*, and the other in AD 6 after Rome deposed Herod Archelaus and annexed and governed Judea directly).

This means that the order of Roman governors was Varus (4 BC)/Quirinius (3 BC and 2 BC)/Varus again.

But, wait a minute here; we *also* know that Gaius Caesar became governor in 1 BC, so how could Varus *possibly* have been governor a second time—the *Lapis Tiburtinus* of 1784 notwithstanding?

The answer may lie with considering who Gaius Caesar was.

Gaius Caesar was a *big shot*. He was the Emperor Augustus' most beloved, and oldest living grandson. He was currently the heir apparent to become emperor after Augustus died. He was *royalty*.

Josephus says that Gaius Caesar was in Rome after Herod died, and that would seem to make perfect sense, since Caesar was one of the two consuls for the year AD 1, whereas certain Roman sources say Caesar was made governor of Syria in 1 BC.[35]

However, this is really no objection at all, because there is no reason why he couldn't have been both.

Robert Graves[36] notes that when Caesar was on his way to his station, he stopped on Chios, met his step-uncle Tiberius, and agreed to take a letter back to Rome for Tiberius.

Dio Cassius notes[37] that the Parthians came to terms with the Romans in AD 1, thereby making the governorship of Syria an easy, peaceful one, thereby allowing Caesar to slip back home to Rome for a visit, and to resume his other duties as consul.

Absentee governors were tolerated if they were important enough. A few decades previously, Pompey had been an absentee governor of Spain for several years, and allowed to rule his province from Rome, sending out viceroys to govern in his absence.

Knowing that Gaius Caesar was a consul of Rome as well as governor of Syria in AD 1; knowing that he did return to Rome at least once in any event, it's easy to place him in Rome after Herod died.

So, this then begs the question: When Gaius Caesar wasn't minding the shop in Syria who was?

Here is where Publius Quinctilius Varus comes into the picture. He was *twice* a governor of Syria, one of those times being after 4 BC, according to the *Lapis Tiburtinus, and* (acting) governor of Syria when Herod died, to believe Josephus. He must have substituted for the sometimes-absent Gaius Caesar (who, in addition, was hardly twenty years old; Augustus would not have objected to having an *experienced* governor while his stripling grandson gallivanted back and forth). It all fits together.

Finally, we have the small matter of dealing with Josephus *seeming* to state that the surviving sons of Herod assumed their tetrarchies in 4 BC after he died.

Dr. Pratt already discusses the reasonable possibility of antedating their regnal years in his paper.

But there is an even stronger argument to make against Josephus' assertion—the witness against Josephus, again being Josephus himself. Or, perhaps more to the point, variant versions of Josephus.

In *Antiquities 18.106*, Josephus states that Herod Philip died in the twentieth year of the reign of the Emperor Tiberius, after having served as tetrarch for thirty-seven years. Since Tiberius came to power in AD 14, that means Philip died in AD 33 or AD 34, which places the commencement or his tetrarchy in 4 BC or 3 BC.

However, Finegan[38] states as follows:

> ... Already in the nineteenth century Florian Riess reported that the Franciscan monk Molkenbuhr claimed to have seen a 1517 Parisian copy of Josephus and an 1841 Venetian copy, in each of which the rest read "the twenty-second year of Tiberius." The antiquity of this reading has now been abundantly confirmed. In 1995 David W. Breyer reported to the Society for Biblical Literature his personal examination in the British Museum of forty-six editions of Josephus' *Antiquities* published before 1700, among which twenty-seven texts, all but three published before 1544, read "twenty-second year of Tiberius," while not a single edition published prior to 1544 read "twentieth year of Tiberius."[39] Likewise, in the Library of Congress, five more editions read the "twenty-second year," while none prior to 1544 records the "twentieth year." It was also found that the oldest versions of the text give various length of reign for Philip of 32 and 36 years. But if we allow for a full thirty-seven year reign, then "the twenty-second year of Tiberius" (AD 35/36) points to 1 BC . . . as the year of the death of Herod.[40]

Summary

The date of Jesus' birth has long been thought to have been in 6 BC–4 BC, based chiefly on evidence left in the writings of Flavius Josephus, which include his report that a lunar eclipse shortly preceded King Herod's death, which therefore has long been thought to have occurred in 4 BC, since a lunar eclipse occurred on March 13, 4 BC.

However, both Josephus and this eclipse are now shown to be weak, untenable, unreliable evidence of these dates, and another time for Herod's date must be found and assigned if possible.

- Josephus himself contradicts his own dates repeatedly, leaving us uncertain about *all* of his dates, including his date of 4 BC, which now is highly dubious.
- Different versions of Josephus exist which add to the uncertainty, in that they give different years for the death of one of Herod's sons, which therefore casts into question the traditional belief that Josephus left behind reliable information to the effect that they began their tetrarchies in 4 BC–3 BC.
- Publius Quinctilius Varus appears to have been twice the governor of Syria, one of those times after 4 BC; Josephus says he was governor when King
- Herod died. Since he couldn't have been governor in 3 BC–2 BC, this leaves him as a perhaps sometime-viceroy, filling in for the sometimes absent Governor Gaius Caesar starting in 1 BC, which therefore is when Herod died.
- There were two Roman *censi* in the final decade of the BC era. One was in 8 BC. While Tertullian believed this was the census mentioned in the Gospel of Luke, this cannot be so, because Quirinius was not the governor of Syria in that year, and because this census counted only Roman citizens. The Holy Family, like almost all the residents of Judea, were not Roman citizens and so wouldn't have been affected by this census. However, the census/registration which occurred in 2 BC as a consequence of the senate and Roman people naming Caesar Augustus the *Pater Patriae*, the "Father of the Country," *would* have affected the residents of the Holy Land since all were required to affirm Augustus in his title. In any event, since Herod didn't die after 8 BC, and since

he did die after *a* census, therefore he could *not* have died in 4 BC.

- Most of the ancient sources (who were much closer in time to the events than we are) believed Jesus was born between 3 BC–AD 1.

- As for the reigns of Herod's surviving sons commencing in 4 BC, in addition to the real existence of differing versions of Josephus' text which places the timing of the commencement of Herod Philip's tetrarchy into doubt, there is also reason to suppose these reigns were antedated in any event; therefore, we cannot rely on information from Josephus to pin down when his sons commenced being tetrarchs.

- Flavius Josephus himself said that King Herod captured Jerusalem and executed his rival for the Jewish throne on the Day of Atonement, also the exact anniversary of the capture of Jerusalem by Pompey twenty-seven years earlier, which was 63 BC, which means, even if he only reigned for 34 years thereafter, he therefore must have died in 2 BC or 1 BC.

- In addition to Josephus' shaky, unreliable timetables, another reason for placing the death of Herod in 4 BC has always been due to the lunar eclipse which appeared over Jerusalem on March 13, 4 BC, because Josephus said a lunar eclipse appeared shortly before King Herod died. However, this eclipse too may be disregarded, along with Josephus' unreliable dates, because it was nothing more than a minor partial eclipse, which furthermore appeared at a very late hour when next to nobody would have seen it.

- Since there were no lunar eclipses in 3 BC or 2 BC, but there were *two* in 1 BC, *one* of these eclipses *has* to be the eclipse that Josephus says heralded the death of Herod. The first eclipse occurred on January 10, 1 BC, and was a full-blown total eclipse of the moon. While this eclipse is suitable because it gives three months between its occurrence and Passover, which gives enough time for a number of significant events to occur (three months, not one month), this eclipse may not be the eclipse of Josephus because it too occurred at a later hour, and moreover at a time of the year when people went to bed even earlier than at other times of the year, and moreover when it can be cold at night in Jerusalem, which would tend to reduce even more the number of viewers.

- Which leaves us with the partial eclipse of December 29, 1 BC, twelve lunar months later. In terms of allowing enough time for certain significant events to occur (again, three months), this eclipse is ideally suited to be the eclipse which Josephus had in mind when he said an eclipse heralded the pending death of King Herod, in that the full moon which rose that night was already under half-umbral eclipse when the moon rose at sunset, thereby assuring that many people would have seen it, many more than the eclipse of January 10. The vote here is that this is the eclipse Josephus had in mind as heralding the death of King Herod, though apart from the issue of how many people saw it, the other eclipse works well too.

- Finally, the major gap in the Gospels separating Luke's account from Matthew's account has been resolved and eliminated! We have long supposed that Luke's Gospel requires Jesus to have been born after AD 6, whereas Matthew's Gospel requires Jesus to have been born between 6 BC–4 BC. However, thanks to understanding Josephus' errors and understanding more about the *Pater Patriae* registration of the entire Roman Empire in 2 BC, this allows us to bridge the ten-to-twelve–year gap between Matthew and Luke by moving Luke's timeline back eight years and moving forward Matthew's timeline by four to six years, actually causing them to meet and even overlap.

Conclusion

King Herod died, not in 4 BC as commonly believed, but either early in 1 BC before Passover, or early in AD 1, again before Passover. (There was no year 0.)

Two eclipses occurred in 1 BC, on January 10 and December 29. Either of these eclipse are the eclipse Josephus wrote about as heralding the death of King Herod, though the latter December eclipse is more probably Josephus' eclipse since many more people saw it.

If King Herod died in 1 BC, then Jesus was born between 3 BC–1 BC.

If King Herod died in AD 1, Jesus was born between 2 BC–AD 1.

The *Pater Patriae* registration of all inhabitants of the Roman Empire in 2 BC (and not the popularly-believed census of Palestine taken in AD 6) is the census that Luke reported as having occurred when Quirinius was governor of Syria. He was governor in 2 BC as well again in AD 6. It should also be noted that Luke did *not* say that Quirinius was governor when King Herod died; only that he was governor at the time the *Pater Patriae* registration was ordered.

King Herod *had* to have been alive in 2 BC because there was no eclipse that year which could have heralded his death, and because the census was the opening act in the series of events which eventually invoked his slaughter of the Holy Innocents in search of the infant Jesus.

The sixth century monk Dionysios Exiguus was "thisclose" to being exactly correct when he assigned December 25, 1 BC[41] as the birthdate of Jesus.

Given the *Pater Patriae* registration of 2 BC, Jesus was probably born sometime in 1 BC.

Therefore, we are right on track in terms of what the Catholic nuns taught me when I was in the first grade (as mentioned in Chapter 1 above), that Jesus lived for about thirty years before commencing his public ministry in the year 30, leading three years later to his Crucifixion in AD 33.

As hard as he tried to get it right, the estimable Pope Benedict would have done better to leave well enough alone, and accept Dionysios Exiguus' original date of the Nativity as the correct one after all!

CHAPTER 3

WHAT DO WE KNOW ABOUT WHEN JESUS DIED?

The method this book will employ will be to cast as large a net as is reasonable, to catch within all the *possible* years in which Jesus *could* have died. Then, it will examine whatever existing evidence there may be why a particular year should be eliminated.

Sir Dr. Colin J. Humphreys[2] says the logical place to start is with all three of the principal actors in the drama of the Crucifixion. When any of them are absent from the venue, then Jesus could not have been crucified at that time.

The three actors are the Roman Emperor Tiberius, his procurator, Pontius Pilatus, and the *Kohen Gadol*, the Jewish high priest, Caiaphas. Luke 3:1-2 says:

> Now in the fifteenth year of the reign of Tiberius Caesar, Pontius Pilate being governor of Judaea, and Herod being tetrarch of Galilee, and his brother Philip tetrarch[3] of Ituraea and of the region of Trachonitis, and Lysanias the tetrarch of Abilene. Annas and Caiaphas being the high priests[4] . . . [5]

From this point, Luke is off and running, telling us the story of John the Baptist, and Jesus' own baptism in the River Jordan, where Luke marks the beginning of Jesus' public ministry. In Luke 3:23, Luke says that Jesus was "*about*" thirty years of age.

Let us begin by asking, what did Luke *mean* when he said Jesus was "*about*" thirty years of age? Was Jesus 28? Or 33? Did Luke even know?

We will set aside this question for later. For now we will ask, what did Luke *mean* when he spoke about the fifteenth year of the reign of the Emperor Tiberius?

At first blush the answer seems simple. We know that the Emperor Augustus died on August 19, AD 14, so by adding 14 + 15, we come out to AD 29.

But it's not nearly as simple as that. There are questions.

Are we counting inclusively or exclusively? If inclusively, then we have to include AD 14, which makes the fifteenth year of Tiberius' reign AD 28, not AD 29.

Does AD 14 count as a regnal year, since Tiberius took over so late?

Could Luke have been as imprecise about the fifteenth year of Tiberius' reign as he was about Jesus' age when he began his public ministry?

And should we even be counting from AD 14?

According to Suetonius,[6] Tiberius became Augustus' co-regent and colleague after he triumphed in Rome in October, AD 12, so could it be that Luke counted from AD 12, thereby placing the beginning of Jesus' public ministry back to AD 27, or even AD 26?

When preparing the original print version of this book back in 1999, I ran a draft copy by Prof. L. Michael White of the University of Texas, who was kind enough to review it and offer me several suggestions, among which was his stated possibility that Luke was counting from AD 12, and not AD 14.

According to Professor White, he believed that John the Baptist could have begun his own ministry as early as toward the end of the year AD 26. I was happy to adopt that possibility and incorporate it into my booklet—and we will see later how valid that was.

But, what about AD 14?

Dr. Humphreys[7] has laid the matter to rest forever. Luke *was* counting from AD 14. Dr. Humphreys found an illustration of a Roman coin in a publication of the British Museum Press, the coin stating that year 1 of Tiberius' reign was the year 45 from the year of the Battle of Actium, when Gaius Octavius (Augustus) and Marcus Agrippa defeated the combined armies and navies of Marcus Antonius and Queen Cleopatra (September 2, 31 BC). Tiberius *officially* began his reign in AD 14.

Our Calendar

Given our extensive use of modern terminology of dating ancient events, it's necessary to define what these dates mean.

Everybody reading this knows what is meant by "leap year." "Thirty days hath September, April, June, and November. All the rest have thirty-one, save for February which has twenty-eight,"—except once every four years, when February has 29.

As alluded to in Note 41 above in the previous chapter, the convention of counting 365 days in a calendar year, and adding an extra day once every four years, is a convention decreed by Julius Caesar.

Before Caesar became the dictator, the Roman system of measuring years had been in a chaotic, great shambles, literally for *centuries*. The ancient Romans operated with a twelve-month lunar calendar, and were perfectly aware that it was necessary to add a thirteenth month periodically, in order to keep the seasons of the year in line with the calendar months. Because there are about 354 days in a twelve-month lunar calendar, calendars need an extra, thirteenth month added frequently, to maintain agreement between calendar months and the season.

In fact, the present Jewish calendar, which is highly accurate, adds a thirteenth month to years seven times every nineteen years, since nineteen, twelve-month lunar years + seven additional lunar months = 19 solar years.

However, the Romans lacked this sense of Jewish self-discipline. They needed to add an extra month every almost every three years, but did so instead very sloppily and irregularly. Really, it was because Roman politicians never wanted to give their rivals a chance to be in office for more than the duration of twelve lunar months. Rather than maintain consistency with the seasons, they let their calendar go, in certain periods, for as much as five to six months ahead of itself, so December literally could fall within seasonal summer.

To recapitulate Note 41 above, because the actual length of the astronomical year is about eleven to twelve minutes shorter than the civil year of 365 days & 6.0 hours = 1 year, the seasons will advance faster than the civil calendar by about one day every 128 years. Pope Gregory XIII corrected this in the year 1582.

We need not concern ourselves with dates after 1582. Therefore, this book will always use the old Julian calendar when stating its dates.

Furthermore, this book will assume, as a matter of stipulation, that Caesar's leap year was always, and rigidly, applied like clock-work every fourth year. While this wasn't necessarily and always the case historically in the early decades after Caesar instituted his reform, it makes no difference, as long as we all understand how we define it all.

We now may define the range of years in which Jesus certainly was crucified, by defining the years when all three of the afore-mentioned players were active and incumbent in Judea: Emperor Tiberius, *Kohen Gadol* Caiaphas, and Procurator Pontius Pilatus.

- **Tiberius Caesar**: We already learned he began ruling on August 19, AD 14. We also know he died on March 16, AD 37.
- **Caiaphas**: It is generally believe Caiaphas was the *Kohen Gadol* from AD 18- AD 36.
- **Pontius Pilatus**: Tacitus[8] as well as all four Gospels stated that Jesus was crucified while Pilatus was the procurator of Judea. Josephus[9] further says that Pilatus served for ten years, from AD 26–AD 36, being recalled at that time by Vitellius, governor of Syria, to answer to the Emperor Gaius Caligula for certain acts committed against the Samaritans.

At the outset then, the range of years for the Crucifixion is AD 26–AD 36. Jesus *must* have been crucified at some time during this span.

We can easily eliminate the first two years from this time span. In the first place, while Pilatus may have been *appointed* early in AD 26 to be the procurator, he could not have arrived on station until several weeks after Passover in that year, because when travel via ship was required, Roman officials didn't even set out on their trips to their duty stations until after the stormy and rainy season of winter had passed; and thereafter, it still took several weeks of travel to arrive. Pontius Pilatus would have arrived much too late in AD 26 to have sentenced anybody to Crucifixion at that year's Passover.

Furthermore, if John the Baptist didn't begin his own ministry until late in the year AD 26 at the earliest, and if his ministry overlapped that of Jesus but began earlier, then Jesus could not possibly have been crucified as early as AD 27.[10] But in any event, thanks to Dr. Humphreys' Tiberius coin, we may be confident that Luke was counting his fifteen years from AD 14. If he counted inclusively, we come to AD 28 as the earliest year when John the Baptist could have begun his own ministry.

Therefore, as a preliminary range of years of the Crucifixion, we will adopt the period of AD 28-AD 36.

What else can we say about the date of the Crucifixion?

We know from all four Gospels that the Crucifixion occurred on a *Friday*. *And*, we know that it occurred, either on the festival of Passover itself (according to the first three, or Synoptic Gospels) or on the day preceding Passover (according to the Gospel of John). (And, in due course, we will be able to *prove* which of the Gospels were correct.)

A brief word should be said here about *Friday* being the day of the Crucifixion. There are some Christians who believe that Jesus lay in his tomb for a full seventy-two-hour three days and three nights. They base this on a literal interpretation of Matthew 12:40, which says, just as Jonah was in the fish's belly for three days and three nights, so too would the "Son of man" remain in the heart of the earth for three days and three nights.

Now Matthew 28:1 also says that Jesus was already risen from the dead on the first morning after the Sabbath. Mark 16:2 says the same, as does Luke 24:1, and John 20:1. So if Jesus were already up 'n at 'em by Sunday morning, and if Jesus were laid to rest shortly before sundown (say, around 5 P.M.) on the day of the Crucifixion, and if Jesus spent seventy-two hours "in the heart of the earth," then it follows that Jesus was likewise resurrected at around 5 P.M., late on Saturday afternoon, and then more or less hung around for a dozen hours or so, waiting for Mary Magdalene to come visiting early on Sunday morning. This in turn means that Jesus was crucified and buried on *Wednesday* afternoon.

Being as charitable as I can be, the theory is patent nonsense. In the first place, it flies in the face of all Christian tradition.

Secondly, it also contradicts Mark 15:42, which says the evening of the burial occurred shortly before the onset of the Jewish Sabbath (Friday evening). Luke 23:54 concurs.

The evidence of the Gospels is clear. If we allow that Jesus was buried at around 5 P.M. *on a Friday afternoon*, and allow that he resurrected shortly before Mary Magdalene appeared, around 5 A.M. on Sunday morning, then Jesus was "in the heart of the earth" for around thirty-six hours.

So what about the seventy-two hours of Matthew 12:40? Simple. Jesus' prediction should be taken as poetry. Furthermore, portions of days counted as entire days. Rabbi Eleazar ben Azariah[11] said, "A day and a night are an *onah* of time, and a portion of an *onah* counts as a whole *onah*."

In other words, the Sabbath was an entire day; the portion of Friday when Jesus was buried before the commencement of the Sabbath *counted* as an entire day, as did the period of Saturday evening until Sunday morning—and there we have our full "three days and three nights."

This book will therefore stipulate that Jesus was crucified on a Friday.

Summary

Jesus was crucified on a Friday that fell either on Passover or the day before Passover, during the years AD 28–AD 36.

But when was Passover in these years?

To discover this, we need to learn some basics of Judaism 101. This we will do in the following chapter.

CHAPTER 4

A FEW RELEVANT JEWISH LAWS AND THE JEWISH CALENDAR, THEN AND NOW

erhaps the first thing to note is that Jewish days begin and end not at midnight, not at noon, not at sunup, but at *sundown*. This has been true since time immemorial[1] and remains true to this day.

The traditional Jewish justification for days commencing at sundown is found in the Book of Genesis.

> . . . and there was evening, and there was morning, one day . . . and there was evening, and there was morning, a second day . . . and there was evening, and there was morning, a third day . . . and there was evening, and there was morning, a fourth day . . . and there was evening, and there was morning, a fifth day . . . and there was evening, and there was morning, a sixth day.[2]
>
> (Gen. 1:5, 8, 13, 19, 23, 31)

Months in the Jewish calendar at one time depended upon the actual sighting of the crescent new moon in the western sky after sundown (in Jerusalem), which is the current Islamic custom (though in Mecca). This practice was discontinued around the year AD 370, but not for the sake of convenience. Rather, it was

abandoned because the entire system of observation and subsequent
dissemination of the news of the sighting of the new moon, both
inside and outside Israel, to the various communities of the
Diaspora, was in a state of disintegration because of the persecution
and dispersal of the Jewish people, and it became impossible to
inform world Jewry when months began and when they should
commence their holidays. Had the current fixed calendar not been
adopted, Judaism itself might not have survived, because nobody
could have known when to observe holidays.

In the present automatic Jewish calendar, given calendar days of
a given month can fall only on certain days of the week. For example,
the first day of Passover now may fall only on a Friday, Monday,
and Wednesday evenings, and rarely on Saturday evening. It may
never fall on Sunday, Tuesday, or Thursday evenings. That's simply
how the arithmetic of this automatic, self-running calendar works.

However, this was not at all the case in the time of Jesus. In his
day, the first day of any month could fall on *any* given day of the
week, just as the new moon today can fall on any day of the week.

The first day of any lunar month in Hebrew is called *Rosh
Chodesh*, which literally means, "the head of the new [month]."
Chodesh can mean either "new" or "month."

In some Jewish months today, *Rosh Chodesh* lasts one day; in
other months, it lasts two days. But why?

The answer is, the automatically-running calendar is designed
to *mimic* what happened in Jerusalem when they still timed the
beginnings of their months upon observation of the new moon,
and when in some months there was no question about when the
new moon became visible, but in other months was a question as
to which of *two* days it *might* have been. For the question arises, if
months could only commence after the new moon were sighted,
what happened at times when the new moon couldn't be seen due
to inclement weather, maybe for several days on end? This happens
not infrequently even in Israel during winter.

Did the rabbis just keep the old month going thirty, thirty-five, forty days, or however many days were required before somebody could actually and physically see the moon? Certainly not. The rabbis had a very good idea of the length of the moon's synodical month.[3] They knew when it was impossible to see the new moon because it was too close to the sun; they knew when it was possible but not certain to see the new moon, and they knew when the moon was definitely visible, would certainly have been seen, if only the weather had permitted. If, during certain months, on the first particular evening when the rabbis knew they *might* have been able to see the new moon, if, on this particular evening, they didn't see it for whatever reason, they knew for a *certainty* that it *would definitely* be visible in the following evening. Now knowing this, the rabbis sent out their runners all over the known Jewish world to announce that *Rosh Chodesh* had commenced, or would commence, on the following evening.

Passover (*Pesach*) falls in the month of Judaism now calls *Nisan*.[4] Deuteronomy 16:1 says:

> Observe the month of Aviv, and keep the Passover unto the LORD thy God; for in the month of Aviv the LORD they God brought thee forth out of the Egypt by night.

"Aviv" means "spring." (The Israeli city "Tel Aviv" means "Hill of Spring.")

> And the LORD spoke unto Moses and Aaron in the Land of Egypt, saying, "This month [of Aviv] shall be unto you the beginning of months; the first shall it be to you of the months of the year."
> (Ex. 12:1–2, author's comment added)

As we've already noted,[1] the Jews returned from the Babylonian captivity with an entirely new set of names for their months. And that's not all; their very language changed. They went into the captivity speaking Hebrew, but came back speaking Aramaic that, while closely related to Hebrew, is itself *not* Hebrew. This is why certain sections of the Book of Daniel were written in Aramaic, and why Jesus' own vernacular was Aramaic, not Hebrew.

When is Passover? On what day of the month of *Nisan* does it fall?

> In the first month, on the fourteenth day of the month, at dusk,[5] is a Passover unto the LORD. And on the fifteenth day of the same month is the Festival of Unleavened Bread unto the LORD; seven days shall you eat unleavened bread.
>
> (Lev. 23:5–6)

All of the above is a roundabout way of saying, on the fifteenth day of the month, in a calendar in which days begin at the point of sundown.

"In the first day [of the above-mentioned festival of Passover; in other words, the fifteenth day of the first month], a holy convocation shall you have; any servile work you shall not do" (Lev. 23:7, author's comments added). This is an important verse, because it will bear upon whether the events of the Last Supper and the subsequent events of the Crucifixion could have occurred on Passover, or must have occurred on the day *preceding* Passover; in other words, on the fifteenth or the fourteenth day of the first month.

Then there is the matter of the sheaf waving.

> And you shall count unto you, from the morrow after the day of rest [to wit, the fifteenth day of the first month] from the day that you brought the sheaf of the waving[6] seven weeks; complete shall they be, even unto the morrow after the seventh seek shall

you number fifty days; and you shall present a meal-offering unto the Lord . . ."

(Lev. 23:15–16, author's comments added)

This is the Festival of *Shavuot*. It must always fall on the calendar day of the week that is one day later than Passover. In other words, if Passover falls on a Sabbath, Shavuot must fall on a Sunday, etc.

This will be useful in helping to determine in which year was the Crucifixion.

Maimonides' Rule

The questions are, a) when was (or is) the new moon definitely invisible; b) when was the new moon *possibly but not definitely* visible, and c) when was the new moon visible as a matter of definition, even if cloudiness preventing its actual sighting?

There are times when the moon is so close to the sun, at or near the time of new moon, that the sun's glare makes the moon invisible. As it is written in the Talmud,[7] "Of what use is a lit candle on a bright day?" Furthermore, what makes the moon visible to us is the sun's light reflecting from it. But at new moon, the moon only shows its dark side to us.

On average, the moon advances away from (or toward) the sun at the rate of about 12.1 degrees of an arc-circle per day.

Maimonides was a celebrated Jewish scholar who lived in Moorish Spain in the twelfth century. He pondered the situation as presented below:

Having found the moon's longitude and latitude, the Talmudic Rabbis next had to ascertain [see pp. 5 and 112] whether in that position in the heavens the new moon would be visible in the neighborhood of Jerusalem. For, as the beginning of the month was fixed on the accredited evidence of witnesses who reported having seen the new moon soon after sunset on a certain day, it was the duty of the Calendar council not only to test their evidence by strictest cross examination, but also to ascertain, by mathematical calculation, whether the moon could, in fact, be seen at that particular moment at the particular place from which the witnesses came. The following additional data were required to answer this question:

(1) The True Elongation [i.e., the difference in true longitudes of the moon and sun, which Maimonides calls the "first length" follows, in Hebrew letters, "aruch rishon"] and

(2) "The Arc of Vision, i.e., the difference between altitudes between the sun and the moon[8] (author's comments added).

Feldman then quoted Maimonides:

"If," says Maimonides, "the true elongation is no more than 9 degrees, then further calculation is unnecessary, since, with such an elongation, the lunar crescent is so small that it is quite impossible for it to be visible anywhere in Palestine [see p. 177]. If the elongation is greater than 15 degrees, it is equally unnecessary to make any further calculation, since one may be quite sure that the crescent would be so large that – under suitable meteorological conditions – it would not fail to be visible throughout Palestine. It is only for intermediate values of the elongation that further mathematical investigation is necessary."[9]

What did Maimonides mean by "lunar longitude"? He meant, the positioning of the moon along a celestial latitude/longitudinal grid. There are modern ways of expressing this. Today, using the modern terms, one knows exactly where in the sky any given object is, just as one knows the location of any place on earth, if one has the data about latitude and longitude. However, as we can see above, Maimonides was already using our familiar system of 360 degrees in a circle.

Now, let's set up a couple of hypothetical examples.

Example 1: On day x (the evening actually, when day x begins), it is known that the new moon was separated from the sun by 7 degrees at sundown. By definition, it is invisible on that evening, and therefore, the next month cannot commence on that evening. But because the moon will advance about 12.1 degrees of an arc during the following 24 hours, we therefore know that on the following evening, it will be separated from the sun by about 19 degrees. *By definition therefore, it is definitely visible.* No eyewitnesses are required to verify having seen it. The new month is therefore proclaimed to fall on the evening of day x+1.

Example 2: On day x-1, it is known that the new moon is in conjunction with the sun at sundown and cannot be seen. On the following evening, day x, it is known that the moon now has a separation from the sun of about 12 degrees of an arc. *It might be visible, but also might not be.*

On *this* evening, therefore, eyewitnesses were needed to verify whether they had actually seen the new moon. If no kosher witnesses were available, the new month was proclaimed to begin on the following evening, on day x+1.

This is why the modern Jewish calendar sometimes has one-day *Rosh Chodesh* and sometimes two-day *Rosh Chodesh*, for in ancient Judea, in some months it was known that the new moon could only occur on a given evening, but in other months, it might have occurred on one of two evenings. The modern Jewish calendar is designed to mimic the modified ancient technique of direct lunar observation to commence new months.

There are no records from these times, so it's impossible today, in such months, to know whether the new moon was the day before or the day after.

Therefore, when estimating the date of the Crucifixion, it will be necessary to keep this point in mind. In some of the years within the range of the possible years of the Crucifixion, we cannot state with precision which of two days Passover was. Of necessity, this might therefore make the task of finding the proper year of the Crucifixion more difficult.

A short parenthetical note, with a bit of humor, is now in order.

The New Testament speaks at length about the enmity between the Jews and the Samaritans. One way this manifested itself was in the matter of examining the eyewitnesses of the new moon.

The Talmud reports instances of Samaritans who attempted to give false witness that they'd seen the crescent new moon in the evening when in fact they had not. To read the Talmudical texts, the Samaritans lied in order to play malicious pranks on the Jews.

They may have had a more sober purpose than that. According to Dr. Humphreys in his book, who cites other modern scholars, the Samaritans operated with a calendar in which new months commenced on the evening after the moon was in conjunction with the sun. Samaritan months therefore generally commenced, and still do, actually, a day or so before Jewish months. Since they believed they were the authentic form of Judaism, they therefore had an incentive to interfere with what they perceived at the false Jewish holidays.

Conclusion

Since Passover falls on the fifteenth day of the month of *Nisan*, and since there are seven calendar days in every week, it therefore follows that in any given year, Passover must *always* fall on the same day of the week as did the first day of the month of *Nisan*.

Therefore: In any year between AD 28 AD–AD 36 inclusive, when we can prove that the new moon for *Nisan* occurred on (for example) a Monday in a given year, we can therefore rule that year out as a possible year in which Jesus was crucified, since the Gospels say Jesus was crucified on a *Friday* afternoon which was either the fourteenth or fifteenth day of the month of *Nisan*.

This will be the primary tool with which this book will eliminate most of the possible years of the Crucifixion of Jesus.

Summary

- From at least the time of the Babylonian captivity until the present time, Jewish calendar days begin at sundown.
- From at least the time of the Babylonian captivity, several centuries before the birth of Jesus, until about the year AD 360, Jewish calendar months commenced either on the first evening when the thin, crescent new moon was seen in the evening sky to the west of Jerusalem, or when calculations showed that the moon was certainly visible, as a matter of definition, even if inclement weather prevented an actual physical sighting.
- In certain months, the new moon was either sighted or proclaimed to have fallen on only one specific day. In other months, the new month could begin on either of two days, depending upon whether any reliable witnesses had seen the new moon on the first of the two possible evenings. If so, then day A was announced as *Rosh Chodesh*, the first

day of the new month; if not, then day B following was proclaimed as the first day of the new month.

- We are looking for the date of the Crucifixion. As we will see in the next chapter, the Crucifixion of Jesus occurred either on the fourteenth or fifteenth day of the month of *Nisan*, and perhaps also in a year when these dates each could have been either of a given pair of days of the week.

CHAPTER 5

DID THE EVENTS FROM THE LAST SUPPER THROUGH THE CRUCIFIXION AND BURIAL OF JESUS OCCUR ON PASSOVER, OR ON THE DAY BEFORE PASSOVER?

Given that we now know that all of the events of the final day of the (pre-Resurrection) life of Jesus, from the Last Supper through the Crucifixion and burial of Jesus, including the agony in the Garden of Gethsemane and the various trials of Jesus, all took place on the same Jewish calendar day, it is now necessary to ask: *Did all of these events take place on Passover, or on the day preceding Passover?*

In other words, did these events take place on Nisan 14 or Nisan 15? Another way to ask this question is, since we know the Crucifixion occurred on a Friday, it makes a huge difference whether it were Friday Nisan 14 or Friday Nisan 15, since these days cannot fall on a Friday in the same year.

Before we can proceed farther, we must decide which is which, if we can.

The first three Gospels resemble each other in style and content, and are called the Synoptic Gospels. They all agree that the Last Supper was in fact a celebration of the first night of Passover.

> Now the first day of the feast of unleavened bread the disciples
> came to Jesus, saying unto him, Where wilt thou that we prepare
> for thee to eat the passover?
>
> (Matt. 26:17)

This was actually the afternoon prior to the dusk of the first
night of Passover; see the remark below.

> And the first day of unleavened bread, when they killed the
> passover,[1] his disciples said unto him, Where wilt thou that we
> go and prepare that thou may eat the passover?
>
> (Mark 14:12)

Again, this was the afternoon prior to the night of the feast.

> Now the feast of unleavened bread drew nigh, which is called
> the Passover . . . Then came the day of unleavened bread when
> the passover must be killed. And he sent Peter and John, saying,
> Go and prepare us the passover, that we may eat . . . And they
> went, and found as he had said unto them: and they made ready
> the passover.
>
> (Luke 22:1, 7–8, 13)

According to Jewish law, Jews may not eat leavened products
after the beginning of the fifth hour (and may not even possess
such items after the sixth hour) on the day preceding the Passover.[2]
That is why the Gospel passages above could say, "then came the
day of unleavened bread," and by that mean, the last (Jewish) day
preceding the festival celebration itself, which the first three Gospels
went on to portray as the Last Supper.

There can be no doubt that the three Synoptic Gospels all
portray the Last Supper as the *seder* of the first night of Passover.
So if we go by the easy assumption that Jesus was following the
same sunset-to-sunset calendar that everybody else was using, it is

clear that the first Holy Thursday evening, and all the events that followed, through the Crucifixion, occurred on the 15th of Nisan.[3]

But there are gross difficulties with this scenario.

In the first place, the strictures of Jewish law flatly prohibited the transaction of public business on festival days.

All the Gospels take great pains to point out there was an urgency in removing Jesus from the cross before sundown on Friday, because it was not allowed to leave his body dangling through the Sabbath. If this is true—and it certainly is true—then it must equally be true that it could not have happened on the afternoon of the first day of Passover either. This includes the events of the Last Supper and all intermediate events. This is because the law prohibiting servile work on festivals were (and are), in most instances, identical with the laws governing human activity on the Sabbath itself.

Then there is the matter of the various trials of Jesus.

According to the *Mishna*,[4] capital trials had to be held during the day. They had to be held in front of the full Sanhedrin.[5] While they could arrive at a verdict of acquittal on the same day of the trial, they had to pronounce the verdict of guilty on the *following* day. And in any event, it could *never* be in session on a Sabbath or a festival.

All of this constitutes negative evidence that the Synoptics flatly got it wrong, and the Crucifixion therefore could not have occurred on any Thursday evening through Friday afternoon that was also Nisan 15. This is something even Matthew and Mark (softly!) concede:

> And [the Temple authorities] consulted [amongst one another] that they might take Jesus by subtilty, and kill him. But they said, Not on the feast day, lest there be an uproar among the people.
> (Matt. 26:4–5, author's comments added)

> After two days was the feast of the passover, and of unleavened bread: and the chief priests and the scribes sought how they might take him by craft, and put him to death. But they said, Not on the feast day, lest there be an uproar of the people.
>
> (Mark 14:1–2)

It makes absolutely no sense for the temple authorities, first to agree amongst themselves that they couldn't arrest Jesus on the day of the festival, and then proceed to do the very thing they already agreed they could not do. So, therefore, the plain reading of this text appears to be highly doubtful, if not impossible.

Furthermore, we also have other evidence from the New Testament itself (plus the Book of Leviticus) that the Crucifixion had to have occurred on the day *preceding* the festival, or, in other words, on the *fourteenth* day of the first month.

In the first place, Matthew himself offers testimony that the day of the Crucifixion was *not* Passover itself, but instead was the day of Passover's preparation, or the day before. Matthew 27 has just described the interment of Jesus in the tomb. Then verses 62-66 state as follows:

> Now the next day, that followed the day of the preparation, the chief priests and the Pharisees came together unto Pilate, saying, Sir, we remember that that deceiver said, while he was yet alive, After three days I will rise again. Command therefore that the sepulchre be made sure until the third day, lest his disciples come by night, and steal him away, and say unto the people, He is risen from the dead: so the last error shall be worse than the first.

This event could have taken place only on the Sabbath, on Saturday. Therefore, even Matthew is at least confused about whether Friday was the Passover or the day preceding Passover.

And then, the Gospel of John also states emphatically that this was the case and thereby disagrees with the other three Gospels:

> Now before the feast of the passover, when Jesus knew that his hour was come that he should depart out of this world unto the Father, having loved his own which were in the world, he loved them unto the end. And supper [Last Supper] being ended . . .
>
> (John 13:1–2)

The verse says "Before the feast," *not* the feast itself.

> When Pilate therefore heard that saying, he brought Jesus forth, and sat down in the judgment seat in a place that is called the Pavement, but in Hebrew Gab-ba-tha. And it was the preparation of the passover, and about the sixth hour: and he said unto the Jews, Behold your King!
>
> (John 19:13–14)

"It was the preparation of the Passover," *not* the Passover itself.

John's unmistakable designation of the day *preceding* Passover as being the day of the Crucifixion also accounts very well for the frantic, urgent quality which is found in all four of the Gospel accounts. When one thinks of it, one must be impressed by the desperate speed that the authorities employed to execute Jesus, once they'd made up their minds to do so. As we saw above, such trials as described were absolutely illegal. Furthermore, it was impossible to try Jesus on the day (night) of the festival itself.

Furthermore, there is the issue of why the authorities would contradict themselves. Having just agreed that they couldn't try Jesus on the festival lest it cause an uproar among the people, the three Synoptic Gospels then state that the authorities then did the one thing they'd agreed they couldn't do.

The whole notion of having to try Jesus, then crucify him, and do it in a rush because the Sabbath was imminent, is simply preposterous. All they needed to do was wait a day, and the Sabbath would be over, and they'd have all the time they wanted.

But, if we understand they had to act fast because Passover also was coming, and in this year in fact coincided with the Sabbath, and with every passing hour more and more pilgrims were converging on Jerusalem, then they simply could not wait until Sunday to do the deed in the presence of potentially thousands of supporters—then we can understand how and why, once they'd made up their minds (at the last minute) that the deed had to be done, why it had to as quickly as possible. In addition to everything else, they had their own Passover ceremonies to prepare and take care of. Finally, the Sadducees were not only secularists, but even on a theoretical basis felt bound by many fewer laws than did the Pharisees, so it might therefore not be surprising to see the priestly class cut a few corners for the sake of doing the job.

It may also be that the authorities thought it urgent to act with haste and be rid of Jesus because they feared Jesus was at the point of fomenting a violent revolution which would bring the Romans down upon their heads.

In such a case, violation of ordinary Jewish law was not only permissible, but even *mandatory*. The rabbinical term is *pikuach ha-nefesh*, and means, "the protection of life." Preservation of life overrides almost all Jewish laws, as Jesus himself said to the Pharisees when they questioned him on why he plucked grain on the Sabbath. Jesus replied that King David had stolen the shewbread when he was being pursued by King Saul and was at the point of starvation, and his starvation justified committing that sin.

At the time of Jesus, the Jews anticipated the arrival of a "Messiah" who would, of necessity, be a martial figure, one who employed violence to achieve his holy ends. Even Jesus' disciples never got this "straight." On numerous occasions, the Gospels state that Jesus chided even the disciples for not understanding that in fact his kingdom was to be a heavenly kingdom.

Jewish history shows this concept at work. In the year AD 132, Shimon bar Kochba (literally, "Simon, the Son of the Star") mounted an armed revolution against the Romans. Rabbi Akiva, the leading rabbi of his age, proclaimed bar Kochba to be the Messiah. Rabbi Akiva later retracted his proclamation that bar Kochba was the Messiah because, after the Emperor Hadrian brutally crushed the revolution, it was apparent that bar Kochba was a false messiah, not a Messiah at all, because the Messiah, by definition, must succeed, and anyone who tries and fails therefore isn't the Messiah.

If even Jesus' own disciples never correctly understood Jesus' mission, then one can surely forgive the temple authorities for believing that Jesus' claims to be the Messiah amounted to a claim to being a *revolutionary, fighting* Messiah, who might well bring a calamity upon the people, as indeed happened twice within the subsequent century.

Their fears of a revolutionary, violent Jesus would have been strengthened by Jesus' own advice to his own disciples to go and arm themselves with swords, and if they lacked money to buy swords, to sell the shirts off their backs to acquire the money.

And then there was Jesus' own evident bad humor during the final couple of weeks before the Crucifixion. For starters, there was Jesus' acid, lengthy, amazing, and intemperate diatribe against the "hypocritical" and "viper-like" Sadducees and Pharisees (Matt. 23:13–16). Then, there was the extraordinary and violent act of chasing the money changers from the temple at the point of a scourging, crying that they'd turned his Father's house into a "den of thieves." In fact, the money changers weren't thieves at all, but instead performed a very necessary and legitimate service to the temple and to the people who needed to change money in order to buy sacrifices.

And then there's the matter of the fig tree. According to the Gospels, Jesus wanted to pick a fig from a fig tree, but found he couldn't, because figs were out of season at the time and the tree had no figs. One would suppose that Jesus should and would have known this, and either should have calmly accepted the absence of a fig, or better yet, shouldn't have tried to reach for a fig he knew, or should have known, wouldn't be there in the first place. But, instead, Jesus petulantly and spitefully cursed the tree and caused it to wither for no purpose at all. *Why* would he *do* that? After all, it wasn't the tree's fault it bore no fruit.

Jesus was very tense and angry that week. Presumably, the authorities had caught wind of this. Combine this specific knowledge with their general knowledge that *anybody* claiming to be the Messiah could be *expected* to lead an armed revolt against the Romans, one can thereby appreciate their motivation and haste to destroy Jesus, after they'd made up their minds that it was necessary.

Let's get back to the issue of whether John's Gospel was correct when it defines the day of the Crucifixion as the day which preceded both the Passover and the Sabbath, which happened to coincide that year.

Let's go ahead seven weeks in time to the following major Jewish pilgrim festival, the Festival of *Shavuot*, or "the Festival of Weeks."

It's well known that the apostles were gathered together in the Upper Room on the occasion of the first Pentecost. Pentecost is synonymous with *Shavuot*, for "Pentecost" means "fiftieth" in Greek, and refers to the fiftieth day following Passover. (It is also the anniversary of *matan torah*, the giving of the Ten Commandments to Moses on Mt. Sinai.)

Recall what was quoted above from the Book of Leviticus. After the first day of Passover, the Jews are commanded to count seven full weeks, a week of weeks. Then, the next day, the fiftieth day, is the day of the festival—hence, *Shavuot*.

As the observant Jews the apostles were (and remained, for decades thereafter, according to Acts of the Apostles), it would have been perfectly natural for the apostles to reunite in Jerusalem at that time, since *Shavuot*, like Passover and *Sukkot*, is one of the three *shalas rogalim*, the three pilgrim festivals, when it was the custom for Jews to travel to, and convene in, Jerusalem.

If Jesus were crucified on Passover (Friday) itself, which is the opinion of the Synoptic Gospels, that would mean that *Shavuot* that year would have had to fall on a Sabbath. If John's Gospel is correct, that would mean *Shavuot* had to fall on a Sunday in the year of the Crucifixion.

Acts of the Apostles itself doesn't specify on which day of the week fell the first Pentecost. But all Christian tradition I've ever encountered states it was on a Sunday. If so, that would mean that the Gospel of John has the right of it, and the day of the Crucifixion was the day preceding Passover.

Summary

All the Gospel accounts agree that Jesus was crucified on Friday afternoon, shortly before the onset of the Jewish Sabbath.

The three Synoptic Gospels claim that this Friday afternoon was first day of Passover itself; the Gospel of John claims that it was the day preceding Passover, which would mean that in the year of the Crucifixion, Passover and the Sabbath coincided. There are numerous difficulties with the Synoptic view. The laws that restrict work and other activities on festivals are (and were) almost identical with the laws that govern such behaviors on the Sabbath itself. The Gospels all state a Jewish scruple about completing the Crucifixion before the onset of the Sabbath. But, surely, the same concerns and objections would have all the events that occurred on Thursday night and Friday too. By defining the Sabbath and the Passover as the same day, the Gospel of John avoids many of these problems.

Furthermore, there is a long-standing Christian tradition that the events of the first Pentecost occurred on a Sunday, which would be possible only in a year in which Passover fell on a Sabbath, so therefore, John probably had the right of it.

Conclusion

At this point, there is no hard conclusion. We will see whether astronomy can now step up and solve the mystery for us, once and for all. But for the moment, we will accept, and live, and work with both possibilities, that Jesus was crucified either on Passover or on the day before.

If Jesus were crucified on Passover itself, that would mean that *Rosh Chodesh*, the first day of the month of *Nisan* in that year, fell on a Friday. If Jesus were crucified on the day before Passover, that would mean that the first day of the month of *Nisan* fell on a Saturday, on a Sabbath.

We have already defined the range of the possible years of the Crucifixion as being between AD 28–AD 36 inclusive. We will eliminate any candidate year in which *Rosh Chodesh* for the month of *Nisan* could not have fallen on a Friday or a Sabbath.

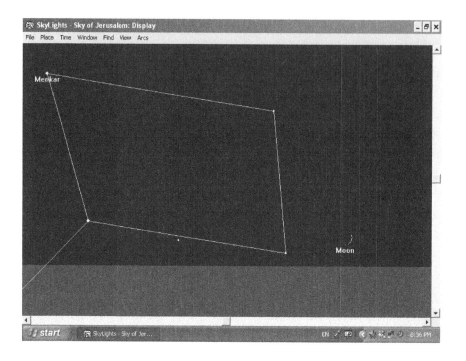

The sky as it appeared on the evening of March 23, AD 30 at moonset, when the new moon for the month of Nisan was barely theoretically visible, since it had an arc of separation from the sun of 9.0 degrees at the time of sunset. The time depicted above is about 6:30 P.M. local time, about a half-hour after sunset. The moon is in the constellation Aries.

Was the moon really visible? Could it possibly have been seen by any observer in Jerusalem?

CHAPTER 6

AD 28–36, THE CANDIDATE YEARS OF THE CRUCIFIXION OF JESUS CHRIST

In Chapter 3, we defined Maimonides' Rule that governed when, how, and/or whether a new moon could be seen in a given month, so that the authorities in Jerusalem could proclaim when that month began. This proclamation would govern on what day of the week any festivals for that month would fall.

To iterate and re-summarize the rule:

When the arc of separation between the sun and the new moon was less than nine degrees of an arc-circle, the moon was, *by definition*, invisible, and therefore *Rosh Chodesh*, the first day of the next lunar month, could *not* be proclaimed;

When the arc of separation between the sun and the new moon was greater than fifteen degrees of an arc-circle, the moon was, *by definition*, visible, and therefore *Rosh Chodesh*, the first day of the next lunar month, *would definitely* be proclaimed, whether or not the new moon had actually been seen by anybody.

When the are of separation between the sun and the moon was greater than nine degrees but less than fifteen degrees of an arc-circle, the moon was, *by definition, possibly visible*. In such cases, which occurred about half the time, the decision whether to proclaim this new day (commencing at sunset) as the first day of the following lunar month depended upon whether any two kosher and reliable witnesses could attest that they'd personally seen the new moon.

We have also defined Passover as the fifteenth day of the month of *Nisan*. This means that in any given year, Passover *must* fall on the same day of the seven-day week as did day one, *Rosh Chodesh*, for the month of *Nisan*. So if we can calculate when day one fell in any given year, we can then easily calculate when Passover fell in that year.

(It may now occur to astute readers, how can I tell which day of the week any of these events fell on? In other words, how can I tell, for example, on which day of the week was March 23, AD 30? My ability to do so is essential to all the following arguments.

(There is a method for calculating on which day any date in history fell. It involves something called "Julian days." Rather than clog up this main text, I'll explain below, in Footnote 1, what "Julian days" are, for the interested readers. Here, it suffices to reassure the reader by remarking that the calculation is easy and certain.)

All times hereafter stated will be in "Jerusalem local standard time." The definition of this can be found in Footnote 2.

Remember, the cardinal rule is any year in which Passover didn't fall on either Friday or Saturday cannot be the year in which Jesus died.

AD 28

Time of new moon:	March 14, 10:42 P.M.
Time of sundown on March 15:	5:55 P.M.
Solar right ascension at sundown:	23h.39m.58s[3]

Lunar right ascension at sundown:	0h.08m.07s
Difference in right ascension in minutes:	28m.09s
Difference in right ascension in degrees:	7.0
Lunar altitude above the horizon:	4 degrees, 44 minutes

Comment: The new moon was definitely invisible on the evening of March 15. It would have been definitely visible, by definition, without or without human observation, since the arc of separation in degrees by the following evening would have been (7.0 + 12.1 = 19.1 degrees).

That means, the new moon would, and could have been proclaimed, for only one single day in this month. Since the evening of March 16 corresponds to March 17, that means that March 17 was day one of the month of *Nisan* in AD 28.

The Julian number for March 17, AD 28 is 1,731,361. When divided by 7, this number yields a remainder of 2.

March 17 was a *Wednesday*. Therefore, Passover that year also fell on a *Wednesday*. *Conclusion:* Jesus could not have been crucified in AD 28.

AD 29

Time of new moon:	April 2, 4:46 P.M.

The moon was definitely invisible at dusk on this day.

Time of sundown on April 3:	6:06 P.M.
Solar right ascension at sundown:	0h.47m.36s
Lunar right ascension at sundown:	1h.24m.59s
Difference in right ascension in minutes:	37m.23s
Difference in right ascension in degrees:	9.3
Lunar altitude above the horizon:	7 degrees, 44 minutes

Comment: Theoretically, the moon was barely visible on the evening of April 3. Probably, nobody saw it. But since this can't be entirely ruled out, it will be necessary to suppose that either April 4 or 5 could have been day one of *Nisan* in AD 29.

The Julian number for April 4, AD 29 is 1,731,744. When divided by 7, this number yields no remainder.

April 4, AD 29 was a Monday; April 5, AD 29 was a *Tuesday*.

Conclusion: Jesus could not have been crucified in AD 29.

30 AD

Time of new moon:	March 22, 6:10 P.M.
The moon was definitely invisible.	
Time of sundown on March 23:	5:59 P.M.
Solar right ascension at sundown:	0h.7m.29s
Lunar right ascension at sundown:	0h.43m.37s
Difference in right ascension in minutes:	36m.8s
Difference in right ascension in degrees:	9.0
Lunar altitude above the horizon:	7 degrees, 47 minutes

Comment: On March 23, AD 30, the new moon was at the theoretical border of invisibility. Based on this fact alone, the chances anybody could see it (see the image which prefaces this chapter) were remote.

But I'm not satisfied to leave it at this point. Frankly, I'd like to eliminate this evening as a candidate for sighting the new moon if I possibly can, and there is a way to do it.

For the new moon to be visible with only 9.0 degrees of arc separation from the sun, it would also have to be as high above the plane of the ecliptic as it ever gets, so as to maximize its elevation over the horizon.

In every orbit the moon makes around the earth, at some point in each orbit it passes about six degrees north of the sun's path (the plane of the ecliptic), and about two weeks later it passes six degrees south.

According to Skylights, the sun's declination, or angle above the earth's equator, was +1.0 degrees; that of the moon was +0.3

degrees. That means the moon was lying about 0.7 degrees *below* the plane of the ecliptic. Since, with only 9.0 degrees of arc separation from the sun, the moon also needed to be about six degrees *above* the plane of the ecliptic, the conclusion therefore is that the new moon was definitely *invisible* on March 23.

However, it was definitely *visible* as a matter of definition on the following evening, since its arc of separation from the sun would have been about twenty-one degrees.

That means that day one of *Nisan* in AD 30 could only have fallen on March 25.

The Julian number for March 25, AD 30 is 1,732,099. When divided by 7, this number yields a remainder of 5.

March 25, AD 30 was a *Saturday*.

Conclusion: Both *Rosh Chodesh Nisan* and Passover fell on Saturday in AD 30.

Therefore, the year AD 30 is an excellent candidate for being the year of the Crucifixion.

AD 31

Time of new moon:	March 11, 7:43 P.M.
Time of sundown on March 12:	5:52 P.M.
Solar right ascension at sundown:	23h.27m.10s
Lunar right ascension at sundown:	23h.57m.52s
Difference in right ascension in minutes:	30m.42s
Difference in right ascension in degrees:	7.7
Lunar altitude above the horizon:	6 degrees, 28 minutes

Comment: This new moon was invisible on March 12, but definitely visible on the following evening as a matter of definition, with or without witnesses. Therefore, day one of this *Nisan* must have been March 14.

The *Julian Number* for March 14, AD 31 is 1,732,453. When divided by 7, this number yields a remainder of 2.

March 14 was a *Wednesday*. So too was Passover.*Conclusion:* Jesus could not have been crucified in AD 31.

AD 32

Time of new moon:	March 29, 9:43 P.M.
Time of sundown on March 30:	6:04 P.M.
Solar right ascension at sundown:	0h.34m20s
Lunar right ascension at sundown:	1h.06m.33s
Difference in right ascension in minutes:	32m.13s
Difference in right ascension in degrees:	8.0
Lunar altitude above the horizon:	8 degrees, 34 minutes

Comment: The comment is the same as for the previous year. The moon was invisible on March 30, but unequivocally visible on the evening of March 31, even without witnesses. April 1 must be day one of *Nisan* for AD 32.

The Julian number for April 1, AD 32 is 1,732,837. When divided by 7, this number yields a remainder of 1.

April 1 was a *Tuesday*.

Conclusion: Jesus could not have been crucified in AD 32.

33 AD

Time of new moon:	March 19, 12:21 P.M.
Time of sundown on March 19:	17:57
Elevation of new moon above horizon at sundown on March 19:	0 degrees, 8 minutes
Comment: The moon was definitely invisible after sundown on March 19.	
Solar right ascension at sundown on March 20:	23h.57m.41s
Lunar right ascension at sundown on March 20:	0h.50m.42s
Difference in right ascension in minutes:	53m.01s
Difference in right ascension in degrees:	13.3
Lunar altitude above the horizon:	13 degrees, 39 minutes

The moon's presence on the north side of the plane of the ecliptic accounts for the minor difference between this value and its right ascension from the sun.

Comment: This is, of course, the year that Christian tradition holds is the year of the Crucifixion. The new moon was probably seen on this evening. But since we're sticking with Maimonides' Rule, we'll withhold certainty and will merely say that March 21 or 22 could have been day one of the month of Nisan in AD 33.

The Julian number for March 21, AD 33 is 1,733,191. When divided by 7, this number yields a remainder of 5.

March 21 was a Saturday.

March 22 was a Sunday.

Conclusion: In this year, Passover probably fell on a Saturday. AD 33 is an excellent candidate. Jesus definitely could have been crucified in AD 33.

AD 34

Time of new moon on March 9:	04:00 A.M.
Time of sundown on March 9:	5:51 P.M.
Solar right ascension at sundown:	23h.17m.24s
Lunar right ascension at sundown:	23h.35m.11s
Difference in right ascension in minutes:	17m.47s
Difference in right ascension in degrees:	4.4
Lunar altitude above the horizon:	5 degrees, 17 minutes

Comment: The new moon was definitely invisible on the evening of March 9, and was definitely visible as a matter of definition on the following evening. Therefore, day one of the month of Nisan for AD 34 was March 11.

The Julian number for March 11, AD 34 is 1,733,546. When divided by 7, this number yields a remainder of 3.

March 11, AD 34 was a Thursday.

Conclusion: Jesus could not have been crucified in AD 34.

AD 35

Time of new moon:	March 28, 07:01 A.M.
Time of sundown on March 28:	6:02 P.M.
Solar right ascension at sundown:	0h.24m.35s
Lunar right ascension at sundown:	0h.36m.04s
Difference in right ascension in minutes:	11m.29s
Difference in right ascension in degrees:	2.9

Comment: The moon was invisible on the evening of March 28.

Time of sundown on March 29:	6:03 P.M.
Solar right ascension at sundown:	0h.28m.03s
Lunar right ascension at sundown:	1h.29m.54s
Difference in right ascension in minutes:	1h.01m.51s
Difference in right ascension in degrees:	15.5
Lunar altitude above the horizon:	19 degrees, 6 minutes

Comment: The new moon was definitely visible on the evening of March 29. Therefore, day one of *Nisan* for AD 35 was March 30.

The Julian number for March 30, AD 35 is 1,733,930. When divided by 7, this number yields a remainder of 2.

March 30, AD 35 was a *Wednesday*.

Conclusion: Jesus was not crucified in AD 35.

AD 36

Time of new moon:	March 16, 9:56 P.M.
Time of sundown on March 17:	5:56 P.M.
Solar right ascension at sundown:	23h.48m.03s
Lunar right ascension at sundown:	0h.18m.29s
Difference in right ascension in minutes:	30m.26s
Difference in right ascension in degrees:	7.6
Lunar altitude above the horizon:	11 degrees, 2 minutes

Comment: The moon was invisible on the evening of March 17. It was, however, visible as a matter of definition on the following evening. Therefore, day one of *Nisan*, AD 36, was March 19.

The Julian number for March 19, AD 36 is 1,734,285. When divided by 7, this number yields no remainder. Therefore, March 19, AD 36 was a *Monday*.

Conclusion: Jesus was not crucified in AD 36.

Summary

Year (AD)	Date of 1 *Nisan*	Date of Passover (15 *Nisan*)	Day of the Week
28	March 17	March 31	Wednesday
29	April 4 or 5	April 18 or 19	Monday or Tuesday
30	March 25	April 8	Saturday
31	March 14	March 28	Wednesday
32	April 1	April 15	Tuesday
33	March 21 or 22	April 4 or 5	Saturday or Sunday
34	March 11	March 25	Thursday
35	March 30	April 13	Wednesday
36	March 19	April 2	Monday

Where's Friday?

We are looking for any year on which Passover (15 Nisan) fell either on a Friday (the Synoptic Gospels) or on a Saturday (Gospel of John). That's because Jewish days ran from the previous evening, either Thursday (Synoptics) or Friday (John) evening. Since a plain reading of the Synoptic Gospels requires that all the events of the Passion, from the Last Supper through the Crucifixion, occurred on the Day of the Passover, which was the day *before* the Sabbath—Thursday evening through Friday afternoon—we therefore are looking for any year in which Passover fell on a Friday.

But, the above table shows no such occurrence of Passover.

Passover *never* fell on a Friday in *any* of the possible years of the Crucifixion of Jesus.

Matthew, Mark, and Luke were simply *wrong* when they said that the Last Supper was a celebration of the Passover *and* implied strongly that it fell on Thursday night.

Astronomy by itself now has *proven* this.

Let us therefore, now and for all time, dispense with this traditional idea forever. The Last Supper simply did not and *could* not occur on a Thursday evening that was also Passover, because Passover never fell on a Thursday evening in *any* of the possible years of the Crucifixion.[4]

The Gospel of John must simply have had the right of it—Jesus was crucified on a Friday that immediately *preceded* the Sabbath, which that year also coincided with the Passover.

Summary

- We already stated that Jesus was crucified on a Friday that either fell on Passover (according to the Synoptic Gospels) or on the day before Passover (according to the Gospel of John).
- We also stated this therefore would have to correspond either with the fourteenth day of the Jewish month of *Nisan* (Synoptic Gospels) or with 15 *Nisan* (Gospel of John), and that these days of *Nisan* could be calculated astronomically, since they depended upon the date of the first appearance of the new moon.
- We have eliminated all possibility that the day of the Crucifixion was Passover itself, since in no year in the range of possible years of the Crucifixion did Passover ever fall on a Friday.

Conclusion: We have found two years in which Passover could have fallen on a Saturday, AD 30 and AD 33.

In the case of AD 30, Passover certainly fell on Saturday, the Sabbath. In AD 33, Passover very likely fell on Saturday the Sabbath, though the following day cannot be entirely ruled out.

Is it possible to narrow it down to one of these two days? The answer is yes! But before we do, it will be useful to review what Jewish prophecy said, and what the Jewish people in the first century AD and Jesus himself believed about the coming of the Messiah.

CHAPTER 7

WHAT DID JEWISH PROPHECY SAY ABOUT THE COMING OF THE MESSIAH?

What did the Jewish people in the first century, Jesus' disciples, and Jesus himself, believe about the coming of the Messiah?

Why was Jesus in the Garden of Gethsemane before the night of the Crucifixion? According to tradition and a plain reading of the Gospels, Jesus was blithely waiting for the temple authorities to come and arrest him, and commence the chain of events that, according to the Gospels, he *knew* would inevitably lead to his crucifixion.

But why wait in the garden itself? If all Jesus wants is to be arrested, why bother going to garden at all? Why not have Judas simply go to the temple authorities and lead Jesus right back to where the Last Supper was held? Or maybe better yet, if Jesus wanted to be arrested so that he could be crucified and atone for the sins of the world, which was the whole point of the exercise, why not simply *present himself* to the temple authorities voluntarily. As in our times, when someone knows there's a warrant out for his arrest, he saves everybody the trouble of finding him by turning himself in to the nearest police station.

The answers to these and other, related questions, may be better appreciated when one understands what Jewish prophecy says about the coming of the Messiah, and what the expectations of the Jewish people and Jesus' own disciples (and, arguably, Jesus himself) were in the first century AD.

The Messiah—who or what is the "Messiah"? What was commonly believed about the Messiah in first century Judea?

A "messiah" is nothing more than a duly anointed, recognized king. King David was a "messiah." So too was King Solomon, and all the kings of Judea, through the time of the exile into Babylon. Even the wicked kings of Judea were still "messiahs," in that they were descendants in the male line from King David, and they all had been duly anointed.

The "messiah" became a king via anointing with oil. That is to say, oil was poured over his head, generally by a recognized prophet, such as Samuel. "Zadok the Priest and Nathan the Prophet anointed Solomon, King," go the words to the marvelous "Coronation Anthem" by Händel, which is sung on every occasion when Great Britain anoints a new king or queen.

To the Jews of the first century (and indeed, unto this day), a "messiah" was nothing more than a king who was blessed and chosen by God, *but was not himself divine.*

The predominant view was that the messiah had to be a descendant of King David in the male line. The purpose of the genealogies of Jesus in Matthew and Luke is to show and prove that Jesus was indeed such a legitimate descendant of King David, and therefore eligible to be the messiah. (That both genealogies admit that Joseph, a man whom the Gospels allege was a true "son of David," was *not* Jesus' natural father, is an issue we need not explore here.)

When Jesus triumphantly entered Jerusalem on what we now call "Palm Sunday," the crowd cried to him as "Son of David"—their way of proclaiming him to be a legitimate messiah.

"*Maschiach ben David,*" the predominant belief, was not the only messianic belief.

There were those who believed in a coming "*Maschiach ben Joseph,*" "Messiah, Son of Joseph." Others still believed in "*Maschiach ben Aharon*" (Aaron). Especially after the brutal suppression of the second Jewish revolt (AD 132–135), there were those who believed that a suffering Messiah, Son of Joseph, had to fight and die, before the Messiah, Son of David could or would emerge.

I think it possible that this Jewish belief in a Messiah, Son of Joseph, the suffering Messiah, could have been influenced by the emerging Christian doctrine of Jesus as a suffering Messiah. Certainly too, this view of the messiah could have been influenced by the bloody failure of the bar Kochba revolt of AD 132–135, in which Rabbi Akiva, the leading Jewish sage of the time, publicly, and mistakenly, proclaimed bar Kochba to be the Messiah.

Revolution in Judea, and the Disciples' Expectations of an Earthly, Militant Messiah

There were numerous other armed revolts against Roman authority in the two centuries or so after the Roman general, Pompey, first made his appearance in Jerusalem.

Both Josephus and Acts of the Apostles 5 mention a revolt by Theudas and Judas the Galilean. Both of these men styled themselves as the messiah, and both attracted a following.

Acts 21 also mentions yet another would-be messiah, someone called "the Egyptian."

There was yet another, albeit lesser known, Jewish revolt which occurred around the year AD 115, which the Emperor Trajan suppressed with typical Roman vigor, not only in Judea, but also on the island of Cyprus. According to Mark Wischnitzer in his book, *Die Juden in der Welt* ("The Jews of the World"), all the Jewish inhabitants of Cyprus were either exterminated *in situ* or were sold into slavery and expelled from the island.

And then, of course, most of all, was the granddaddy of all the Jewish revolts, the revolt of AD 66–73. This revolt was led by what we might anachronistically call a group of "extreme right-wing" Pharisees called the "Zealots," who weren't content to wait for the Messiah to come and lead the Jewish people into independence in his own good time, but rather who thought it better to take matters into their own hands without waiting for any messiah to lead them. Indeed, some of the Zealots were *republican* in sentiment, wanting *no king whatsoever*, not even a son of David. In fact, some of them killed their own leader when, at the outset of the revolt, he proclaimed himself to be their messiah. In Jewish history, there is considerable anti-monarchial sentiment, as a study of the book of Judges and the books of Samuel will show.[1]

Judea was a hotbed of revolutionary sentiment throughout the first 200 years or so of Roman influence (63 BC–AD 135), with the people fervently wishing for an *earthly* messiah to come and restore Jewish independence.

They'd have been totally baffled by the present Christian concept of a heavenly Messiah, one who indeed did come, but left the structure of his (and their) world unaltered, and who promised to return (and complete his messianic work), but up to 2,000 years or even more in the future!

The Disciples as Revolutionaries?

Jesus, of course, was from Galilee, and moreover recruited all his disciples from Galilee. Given what was said above, the disciples could be excused for sharing the general Jewish expectation of the rise of an earthly, militant messiah.

Galilee was a region known for its anti-Roman revolutionary fervor. Judas the Galilean was from Galilee, and the revolt of AD 66 broke out in Galilee (today's northern Israel).

At least four of Jesus' twelve disciples were revolutionaries!

This may surprise many readers. The Gospels tend to understate and minimize this, but, nevertheless, traces of this can be found even in the Gospels.

Mark 3:17 refers to James and John, sons of Zebedee, as the Sons of Thunder. That is a street name like "Puff Daddy" or "Snoop Dogg," if I ever heard one.

Luke 6:15 refers to Simon the Zealot, a member of the Pharisee party that believed in armed revolt against Rome.[2]

And then there's the most famous Zealot of them all—*Judas Iscariot.*

Judas Iscariot

Did any readers ever wonder why he's the only named disciple who has a family-sounding surname, like "Judas Jones," so to speak?

Except, it's *not* a family name, or surname, or a "last name." Rather, "Iscariot" is a *street-name*, like "Mack the Knife" or "Grandmaster Flash."

"Iscariot" is a combined, composite name, with an Aramaic and a Latin element. Basically, it means *Judas the Daggerman.*

Here's how it works: In Hebrew and Aramaic, *ish* means, simply, "man." *Ish,* "man;" *isha,* "woman."

The Latin element is *sicarius. Sicarius* is an interesting word, in that it is a word whose original meaning is "dagger." It was borrowed and altered by the Zealots who, according to Josephus, employed *sicarii* (literally, "daggers") to assassinate Romans, and who were so named because they assassinated their Roman victims by sneaking up on them and killing them with *dagger*-thrusts. This altered meaning then made its way back into Latin and persists to this day in places like Sicily and Mexico,[3] where the word *sicario* still means "assassin."

Certain words, original to a given language, have been known to make a trip to other languages, and then return to its original language in altered form. "Assassin" itself is one such word. Originally in Arabic, it simply meant "hashish." But in the Middle Ages in the Middle East the deadly cult of the Assassins arose, whose killers were inspired to kill fearlessly after being doped-up on hashish.

(And then there's the word "robot." In Russian/Polish, the word *robota* simply means "work." But early in the twentieth century, American science fiction writers borrowed the word to refer to soulless mechanical men, perhaps reflecting their sense that the USSR was a place with millions of soulless working masses. Anyway, the word "robot," without the feminine ending "a," has made its way back to Russian and Polish to mean a tireless, programmed, soulless self-directed machine.)

The word *sicarius* itself has also been altered to refer to certain smoking products! If one strips away the *ius* ending, one is left with *sicar*, which is basically the same thing as "cigar." A "cigar" is a cigar because of its *dagger* shape. If one adds the French diminutive *ette* to "cigar" (such as in "Marie Antoin-ette," "Marie Little-Antonia"), one gets "cigarette," which really means "little cigar."

Anyway, getting back to Judas *Iscariot*: when one also keeps in mind that the *ot* ending in Hebrew is used for the plural form of most feminine and certain masculine nouns, what we then have is "Judas Ish-sicariot," or "Judas Man-daggers," or "Judas, the Man of Daggers," or "Judas the Daggerman."

So Judas was not only Galilean, not only a Zealot, but was also a *sicarius*, one of the Zealots' killers.

Odd indeed that he, of *all* people, would become one of the Twelve, the closest of all Jesus' followers! Even odder that *he*, of *all* the disciples, would "betray" his own master to the very temple authorities whom all Zealots loathed as Roman lackeys.[4]

In summary, we have arguably four of Jesus' twelve disciples who were so keen to oust the Romans from Judea "by any means necessary" (to quote the late American-Muslim firebrand Malcolm X) that they were publicly notorious for it.

Which then begs the next question: Was Jesus himself an advocate of physical rebellion against the Romans in order to usher in the Messianic Age? Or was he, the ever-peaceful Messiah, who was never understood, not even by his own disciples?

This will be startling to many who read these words, since the universal picture of Jesus is that of a man of non-violent, pacifistic tendencies which surpass those of Mahatma Ghandi. Jesus *is* the "Prince of Peace." His true kingdom is not an earthly kingdom of violence, but is rather, and against all contemporaneous expectations, an other worldly, heavenly kingdom of peace and bliss.

- Matthew 5:39 quotes Jesus, "But I say unto you, That ye resist not evil: but whoever shall smite thee on thy right check, turn to him the other also [so that he may strike that cheek too]" (author's comment added).
- Matthew 5:44: "Love your enemies, bless them that curse you, do good to them that hate you, and pray for them which despitefully use you, and persecute you."

Then there are all the times throughout the New Testament when Jesus reproves his disciples for expecting an earthly, militant messiah, when his own kingdom was "not of this world" and was totally different in character.

- Mark 8:18: "Having eyes, see ye not? and having ears, hear ye not? and do ye not remember?"
- Mark 9:31-32: "For he taught his disciples, and said unto them, The Son of man is delivered into the hands of men, and they shall kill him; and after that he is killed, he shall

rise the third day. But they understood not that saying, and were afraid to ask him."

- Luke 18:31-34: "Then he took unto him the twelve, and said unto them, Behold, we go up to Jerusalem, and all things that are written by the prophets concerning the Son of man shall be accomplished. For he shall be delivered unto the Gentiles, and shall be mocked, and spitefully entreated, and spitted on. And they shall scourge him, and put him to death: and the third day he shall rise again.And they understood none of these things: and this saying was hid from them, neither knew they the things which were spoken."

- Luke 19:11: "And as they heard these things, he added and spake a parable, because he was nigh to Jerusalem, and because they thought that the kingdom of God should immediately appear."

  (The Jews in general believed this would happen if a militant messiah, such as Bar Kochba, 100 years later, were to arise to usher in the Messianic Age *by fighting for it.*)

- John 2:20-21: "'Then said the Jews, Forty and six years was this temple in building, and wilt thou rear it up in three days? But he spake of the temple of his body."

- John 3:9-10: "Nicodemus answered and said unto him, How can these things be? Jesus answered and said unto him, Art thou a master of Israel, and knowest not these things?"

- John 4:31-34: "In the mean while his disciples prayed him, saying, Master, eat.But he said unto them, I have meat to eat that ye know not of. Therefore said the disciples one to another, Hath any man brought him ought to eat? Jesus saith unto them, My meat is to do the will of him that sent me, and to finish his work."

  (But, of course, the disciples had no concept of this extraordinarily extra-worldly thought, and were unable to think past the dinner table.)

- John 6:53-60: presents Jesus' long discourse about the meaning of eating his flesh and blood. Then in verses 60-61: "Many therefore of his disciples, when they had heard this, said, This is a hard saying; who can hear it? When Jesus knew in himself that his disciples murmured at it, he said unto them, Doth this offend you?"

  In the following verses, Jesus then says, in effect, he knew who could not understand these words, and that no one could come unto him, unless it were given unto him by the Father. Then verse 66: "From that time many of his disciples went back, and walked no more with him."

- John 14:5–6: "Thomas said unto him, Lord, we know not whither thou goest; and how can we know the way? Jesus saith unto him, I am the way, the truth, and the life: no man cometh unto the Father but by me."

  (This appears to be the reverse of what Jesus said in John 6:65, when he said, no one could come unto him unless it were first given unto him to do so by the Father.)

  John 14:7: "If ye had known me, ye should have known my Father also . . ."

- John 16:17-18: "Then said some of his disciples among themselves, What is this that he saith unto us, A little while, and ye shall not see me: and again, a little while, and ye shall see me: and, Because I go to the Father. They said therefore, What is this that he saith, A little while? we cannot tell what he saith."

And yet, despite all the above, all the Gospels give hints that even Jesus had his own violent side. We've already seen that several of his closest disciples were Zealots who were dedicated to immediate and violent revolution, as a means to usher in the Messianic Age of bliss and universal peace. Then the Gospels report as follows:

- All the Gospels report that Jesus violently purged the temple of its money changers.
- All three Synoptic Gospels tell the story of the cursing and killing of the fig tree.
- Matthew 10:34–35: "Think not that I am come to send peace on earth: I came not to send peace, but a sword. For I am come to set a man at variance against his father, and the daughter against her mother, and the daughter in law against her mother in law."
- Luke 22:35-38: "And he [Jesus] said unto them, When I sent you without purse, and scrip, and shoes, lacked ye anything? And they said, Nothing. Then said he unto them, But now, he that hath a purse, let him take it, and likewise his scrip: *and he that hath no sword, let him sell his garment, and buy one.* For I say unto you, that this that is written must yet be accomplished in me. And he was reckoned among the transgressors: for the things concerning me have an end. And they said, *Lord, behold, here are two swords.* And he said unto them, *It is enough*" (author's comment and emphasis added).

This last scene took place at the Last Supper, immediately before Jesus and most of the Twelve departed Jerusalem to go to the Garden of Gethsemane.

This is actually going to be a clue into determining whether the date of the Crucifixion was April 7, AD 30, or April 3, AD 33.

Jesus went to the Garden of Gethsemane that night, neither heavily armed nor unarmed. He was *lightly* armed. He foresaw a need to be armed, but *lightly* armed. Jesus, the Prince of Peace, went to the garden *lightly armed. Why* go at all?

Traditional Christian belief is, Jesus went to Golgotha willingly to die via crucifixion and thereby atone for the sins of the whole world. Moreover, he knew, literally for all eternity, this was his mission and his *fate*. The incident in the Garden of Gethsemane would be where the entire drama of the Passion and Crucifixion would commence. Jesus would commence the process by *willingly* submitting to arrest by the temple authorities.

And we *know* that Jesus *willingly* consented to arrest, since we know that Jesus knew that Judas would bring the temple authorities to the garden to arrest him. If he didn't want to be arrested, all he therefore needed to do was not to present himself in the garden.

So then, if Jesus *wanted* to be arrested, then why go to the garden at all, with or without weapons?

We commenced this chapter by asking this question, but I'll ask it again here.

Why bother with Judas and the garden at all? If Jesus wished to be arrested, why not simply march on down to the temple itself and present himself there to the temple authorities? Or why not have Judas tell the temple authorities to come to the room where they had the Last Supper, and where they could still find Jesus?

The Gospels report Jesus prayed for three long hours in the garden itself. But, *why*? At *this* point, the whole matter had been set into motion. There was nothing more to do. There is a fatalistic certainty at this point. The Crucifixion is the most important single event in human history, and now was the time for the show to go on. Generally, when people pray, it's to ask God to reverse an evil decree and turn it into a good decree. The Gospels actually portray Jesus doing precisely this—asking the Father to remove this bitter cup, if it be according to His will.

But *why* bother asking for that which Jesus, according to traditional Christian belief, *knows* is impossible. Why also Jesus' bitter disappointment with the disciples for not sitting up and praying with him? According to traditional Christianity, the Crucifixion is *inevitable*. If so, then what possible difference could the disciples and their prayer make at this juncture?

To answer these question, it will be useful to look at a few Old Testament prophecies which speak to the advent of the Messiah.

There is the famous prophecy from Zechariah 9:9-10 (used by the composer Händel in his famous oratorio *The Messiah*), a prophecy which Jesus consciously fulfilled with the triumphal entry into Jerusalem:

> Rejoice greatly, or daughter of Zion; shout, O daughter of Jerusalem: Behold, thy king cometh unto thee: He is just and having salvation; lowly, and riding upon an ass, and upon a colt the foal of an ass. And I will cut off the chariot from Ephraim, and the horse from Jerusalem, and the battle bow shall be cut off; and he shall speak peace unto the heathen: and his dominion shall be from sea even to sea, and from the river even unto the ends of the earth.

Now, there was nothing magical about Jesus fulfilling the prophecy. It's not like this prophecy were unknown until Jesus did it, and then people later realized what he'd done. No, quite the contrary. This prophecy was already universally known in the Judea ofof the first century. When Jesus rode on donkey back into Jerusalem, it was simply his way of making an official announcement that he was the Messiah, in a manner that would be unmistakable to anybody. It was the equivalent of modern political candidates making their candidacies official by filing candidacy papers with the state-level secretary of state, and holding a press conference and a rally thereafter.

From this it's clear Jesus was a bit of a politician, and was well aware of the need to persuade the people that he had indeed fulfilled numerous Old Testament prophecies concerning the Messiah, and therefore deserved to be regarded by them as being the Messiah.[5] And we have already seen *what kind of Messiah* they were all expecting—an earthly, militant Messiah.[6]

This now brings us to the prophecies of Joel:

The Book of Joel begins by speaking of the decay of the moral fiber of Israel, and then says in verse 6, "For a nation is come unto my land, and without number, and whose teeth are the teeth of a lion, and he hath the cheek teeth of a great lion." *In the first century, this was universally regarded as Rome.*

The book then calls upon the people to repent, fast, and then assemble and resist. Chapter 3 calls upon the Israelites to "beat their plowshares into swords and their pruning forks into spears," in order to become ready for the Day of the Lord. It is an interesting reversal of the Book of Isaiah, which speaks of beating swords into plowshares when the Messianic Age arrives.

Joel 3:19 says, "Egypt shall be a desolation, *and Edom shall be a desolate wilderness.*" I added emphasis there, but *why*? The answer is because, in the first century, it was widely believed that *Edom = Rome*. In the Bible, Esau, the brother of Jacob, was the progenitor of Edom. In the Midrashic literature, Edom is seen as the progenitor of Rome.[7]

The last two verses (Joel 3:20-21) speak of the Messianic Age: "But Judah shall dwell forever, and Jerusalem from generation to generation. For I will cleanse their blood that I have not cleansed, for the LORD dwelleth in Zion."

- Joel 1:15: "Alas for the day! *For the day of the LORD is at hand*, and as a destruction from the Almighty shall it come" (emphasis added).
- Joel 2:1-2: "Blow ye the trumpet in Zion, and sound an alarm in my holy mountain: let all the inhabitants of the land tremble: *for the day of the LORD cometh*, for it is nigh at hand. A day of darkness and of gloominess, a day of clouds and thick darkness . . . " (emphasis added).

- Joel 2:10: "The earth shall quake before them; the heavens shall tremble; *the sun and the moon shall be dark*, and the stars shall withdraw their shining" (emphasis added).
- Joel 2:11: "And the LORD shall utter his voice *before his army*: for his camp is very great; for he is strong that executeth his word, *for the day of the LORD is great*, and very terrible; and who can abide it? (emphasis added).
- Joel 2:31: "*The sun shall be turned into darkness, and the moon into blood, before the great and terrible day of the LORD come*" (emphasis added).
- Joel 3:9: "Proclaim ye among the Gentiles: Prepare war; wake up the mighty men; let all the men of war draw near; let them come up."
- Joel 3:15: "*The sun and the moon shall be darkened*, and the stars shall withdraw their shining" (emphasis added).

To summarize the prophecies here:

Four refer to the "Day of the Lord."

The Day of the Lord is but a *single* day of day and night.

Two prophecies speak of armies, one God's army, the other the Gentiles' army, and they must clash.

Three prophecies state the sun will go dark.

Two prophecies say the *moon* will go dark; the third prophecy says the moon "will turn to blood."

In general, the entire Book of Joel is a book that foretells of widespread catastrophes and destruction, which will all come to a head on the Day of the Lord, and afterward, the Holy Land will become a paradise of peace and happiness.

Summary

In the first century, the Book of Joel was seen as a prophecy of how the Messiah would usher in the Messianic Age. He would do so by going to war against the Romans and throwing them out of the Holy Land.

The book talks about the great battle happening in a single day and night, and would be accompanied by heavenly portents. It would take place inside the Holy Land (in the Valley of Jehoshaphat) and on the "holy mountain." Which mountain was that? Well, the Mount of Olives was handy, since it was next to Jerusalem. There is a rabbinical legend which said that the Messiah is destined to make himself manifest on the Mount of Olives at the end of *Sukkot*.

And with all this, *now* we have a sense of why Jesus was on the Mount of Olives in the Garden of Gethsemane, waiting for the temple authorities to come.

It had to do with Jesus' public proclamation that he was the Messiah. If so, then in order to *be* the Messiah, he had to fulfill the prophecies relevant to being the Messiah.

That included riding into Jerusalem on donkey back. And that included the prophecies related to the Day of the Lord.

The Day of the Lord had to happen on a *mountain*—hence, the Mount of Olives. Inside the city of Jerusalem would not do. That is why Jesus did not have Judas lead the temple authorities back to the building where they'd held the Last Supper.

The time of passive turn-the-other-cheek to evil was over, and the time to take up arms to resist evil was at hand—hence Jesus' words in Luke, where he tells his disciples, at this point, to arm themselves, and to sell the garments off their backs if that is necessary to raise money with which to buy swords.

Jesus went to the Garden of Gethsemane *lightly* armed. Not *un*armed, but also not *heavily* armed. As Jesus said when his disciples told him they could find two swords, *"It is enough."*

But why bring even two swords if Jesus' conscious intent is to surrender meekly to the temple authorities, so they could then commence the process that would end with Jesus' eternally-fated sacrifice on Golgotha? And why bring only *two* swords?

Why not go there *heavily* armed—go there "heavy," as Tony Soprano might have put it, in order to have it out with the temple authorities? Evidently, Jesus intended to put up *some* kind of resistance.

Here are the answers:

To fulfill Messianic prophecy by bringing on the battle which was foretold by the Book of Joel, that must happen on the day the Messiah becomes manifest. Peacefully surrendering to the temple authorities without a struggle didn't fulfill the Messianic requirements of the Book of Joel.

Now, Jesus could not conceivably have believed he could take on the entire Roman Empire by himself, his dozen disciples (even if some were Zealots and Sicarii), and two swords. But obviously, he didn't believe the matter was hopeless, either; else he'd not have attempted it in the first place—or bothered to bring even the two measly swords.

There is both a miraculous and an earthly element to the Book of Joel. The earthly element is its prophecy of a battle between men, with large destruction. Its miraculous element is that the good side wins in spite of incredible odds against it.

So now we see why Jesus went to the garden on the Mount of Olives: because he believed the Day of the Lord had to commence there.

Now we see why Jesus went there *lightly* armed—because he knew that he'd have to wage a real fight on the Day of the Lord, though it need not have been the "Mother of All Battles." But it *did* need to be a *real* fight. Then, at *this* point, God Himself wouldprovide the miracle and do the rest Himself—that is to say, *if* Jesus found favor in his Father's eyes.

This also explains why Jesus prayed as hard as he did. He was praying for greater stakes than anybody in human history ever has, before or since—the ushering in of the Age of the Messiah, with its universal peace, bliss, holiness, and universal service to the One True God.

And Jesus the man *was uncertain of success*. He *hoped* for success. He'd done everything *he* could to bring about success. But worthy would-be messiahs had come and gone before him, and all had failed.

Jesus prayed as intently as he did because maybe, *just* maybe, if the matter were otherwise balanced on a knife's edge, the force of his prayer might, *just* might, tilt and tip the verdict in his favor.

And this was why Jesus was so angry with his disciples for sleeping when they should have been adding the force of their own prayers to His, and maybe help improve the chances for success.

This was why Judas hanged himself, in bitter grief, after seeing that his beloved master not only had failed, but in addition was *definitely* going to wind up on a cross for his trouble—and he was an integral part of that.

For Jesus' pathetic little coup d'état was over before it had barely begun.

For Jesus himself realized rapidly how hopeless and lost his cause was when, after Peter struck off the temple servant's ear, Jesus told him to put his silly sword away.

"Thus the world ends," wrote T. S. Elliot, "not with a bang but with a whimper." And so it was with Jesus' miserable attempt to commence the Day of the Lord—over before it began.

But are we *really* sure of this?

Could it be—could it *just* be, that the Day of the Lord did really happen after all— but in a totally unimaginable, unexpected way?

In the next chapter, modern astronomy may help reveal the answer.

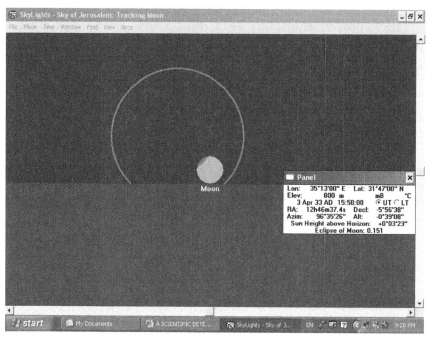

Position of the moon at full moonrise, at 6:15 P.M., on April 3, AD 33

CHAPTER 8

THE LUNAR ECLIPSE OF APRIL 3, AD 33

A few preliminary words are necessary here about the above illustration.

1. The panel in the illustration states a "UT" of 15:58. UT means, universal time, as determined from the meridian which today runs through Greenwich, UK, and which is the basis for modern time zones. Jerusalem is two time zones east of the prime meridian, so in the local time zone, it is really 17:58, or 5:58 P.M. However, Jerusalem lies somewhat east of the center of its time zone, which causes local high noon to fall somewhat earlier than 12:00 mean time. In fact, on this day, local high noon fell at 11:43 A.M. But, since it was the custom in Jesus' time to apportion twelve hours of equal, but proportional length, it is therefore fitting to define local high noon at 12:00, and not 11:43 A.M. This forces me to add seventeen minutes to the times that the computer assigns for all the events which occurred on April 3, AD 33, and therefore, the correct time in this illustration, the point of full moonrise, is not 5:58 P.M. but rather 6:15 P.M.

2. The circle is the full extent of the cone of the earth's shadow. It defines the earth's "penumbral" shadow, that portion of the shadow in which the earth *partially* eclipses the sun. The "umbral" portion of the shadow, in which the earth wholly eclipses the sun, is in the center of the circle, like a bull's eye.

3. Ordinarily, my program depicts the full moon as bright white, but the grayness in this illustration of the full moon reflects the fact that the moon is currently under partial penumbral eclipse, and is therefore not as bright as it ordinarily is.

4. The reader will also note a darker chip in the upper-left corner of the moon. This reflects the fact that this portion of the moon was under the earth's full umbral shadow, where the sun was under total, not partial eclipse. At this point, about fifteen percent of the moon's surface was lying within the earth's umbral shadow, and to a viewer on earth, this chip appears black. And, I should add, the border area of the black chip is blurry and smudgy.

Up to this point, we've determined that Jesus was crucified either on April 7, AD 30 or on April 3, AD 33. This is as far as an analysis of new moons for *Nisan* between AD 28–AD 36 can take us.

We've also seen how Jesus consciously set out to fulfill certain Messianic prophecies, in order to establish to the people that he in fact was the promised Messiah. Among these prophecies was Joel's prophecy about the coming Day of the Lord, the day on which the Messiah would become manifest on earth, which would be marked by a darkening of both the sun and the moon.

So now it's time for astronomy and the New Testament to take us the rest of the way, to see if we can fix one specific date for the Crucifixion of Jesus.

The three Synoptic Gospels all speak of a darkness that fell over the land from the sixth to the ninth hours on the day Jesus was crucified.

> And it was about the sixth hour, and there was a darkness over all the earth until the ninth hour. And the sun was darkened, and the veil of the temple was rent in the midst. And when Jesus had cried with a loud voice, he said, Father, into thy hands I commend my spirit: and having said thus, he gave up the ghost.
>
> (Luke 23:44-46)

Matthew, Mark, and Luke all agree that Jesus "gave up the ghost" and died at around the commencement of the "ninth hour."

Before we go farther, we should define and understand what we mean by any "xth hour."

When most people see the expression "the sixth hour," they think of that as being the same thing as 12 o'clock noon. Even Dr. Humphreys did so in his book *The Mystery of the Last Supper*. And therefore, we ordinarily think of Jesus languishing on the cross from 12 noon–3 P.M. I know when I was a small boy who attended Catholic parochial schools, the nuns encouraged us to emulate Jesus and remain totally silent on Good Friday between 12 noon–3 P.M.

However, I hold that the common sense is erroneous, wrong by a factor of one hour, and here's why:

In those times, throughout the Roman world, the custom was to divide day and night periods into twelve units of equal length.[1] Naturally, in winter, that meant a single "hour" lasted about what we would call forty-five minutes, and in summer, a single hour could last around seventy-five minutes.

The "first hour" of any given day would be what we'd call 6 A.M. In other words, all days, regardless of summer or winter, began "at 6 A.M." That means that the second hour is equivalent to 7 A.M.; the 3rd hour to 8 A.M., etc. This therefore means that if Jesus were crucified from the sixth hour to the ninth hour, that would roughly correspond to 11 A.M.– 2 P.M., not noon–3 P.M., as is commonly thought.

This is the manner of reckoning hours that I have adopted throughout this book. So how long was a proportional hour on April 3, AD 33? That day was 752 minutes long, in other words, a day which lasted twelve modern hours and thirty-two minutes. Which means that a proportional hour on April 3 was slightly longer than what we would call sixty minutes. In fact, a proportional hour on April 3, AD 33 lasted exactly 62 ⅔ minutes, or 62 minutes and 40 seconds.

The evangelists do not say that Jesus was crucified at exactly the commencement of the sixth hour and died exactly at the beginning of the ninth hour. If they had said that, we might therefore want to conclude that Jesus hung on the cross, not for 180 minutes, but instead for 188 minutes, and that Jesus was crucified at exactly 10:57:20 A.M. and died at exactly 2:05:20 P.M.

But as it is, the evangelists were approximate in their estimates of when these events happened. They say, at *about* the xth hour. Exact timekeeping in those days was impossible anyway. For these reasons, and because the difference in the ancient proportional hour for April 3 and its modern version is minor, I have ignored this phenomenon throughout this book, and do so in this chapter, save for the statements below of when the sixth and ninth hours commenced, where I did use proportional hours.

Time of sunrise on April 3, AD 33:	5.27 A.M. (local mean time; GMT+2)
Time of sunset on April 3, AD 33:	5.59 P.M.
Length of daylight on April 3, AD 33:	12 hours, 32 minutes, or 752 minutes
Time of local high noon:	11.43 A.M.

This is the moment when exactly half of the day had lapsed, and when the sun was at its highest. It is also the beginning of the seventh hour of the day.

I define this time as 12:00 high noon. Therefore, all times for this day will be adjusted by adding seventeen minute. On April 3, AD 33, the definition of sunrise will be not 5:27 A.M., but rather 5:44 A.M. Sunset will be not at 5:59 P.M., but rather at 6:16 P.M.

The core argument in this entire book centers around the eclipse of April 3, AD 33. It is the contention of this book that this eclipse *proves* that Jesus was crucified on April 3, AD 33.

This eclipse began at almost the precise moment, as closely as is possible to tell, when Jesus died (if in AD 33), and continued as he was taken down from the cross and was buried.

So now therefore, let us prepare a table of all the astronomical events for this day, other than those already stated above:

Time of commencement of the sixth hour (when Jesus was hoisted on the cross)	10:57 A.M.
Time of commencement of the ninth hour (when Jesus expired; note that in these three proportional hours, 188 minutes lapsed, not the standard 180 minutes)	2:05 P.M.
Time of first penumbral contact[2]	2:15 P.M.
Time of first umbral contact[3]	3:36 P.M.
Time of maximum totality	5:03 P.M.
Percentage of maximum totality	58 percent
Time of full moonrise	6:15 P.M.
Percentage of totality at moonrise[4]	15 percent
Time of last umbral contact:	6:38 P.M.
Eclipse over	7:51 P.M.

Jesus "gave up the ghost" within minutes, perhaps at the very moment, when this eclipse began, as though the very heavens were bearing witness to the event.

What Does This Mean?

It is plain that the inhabitants of Jerusalem would have witnessed a partial, fading eclipse of the moon at the point of moonrise on April 3, AD 33, after Jesus was already interred in the ground, as they were going to wherever they were going to perform the rituals of Passover.

At the very least, the eclipse is an uncanny coincidence.

But to the followers of Jesus who witnessed the Crucifixion, it should have meant a lot more. It should have meant this:

The events of the Crucifixion commenced with the arrest of Jesus in the Garden of Gethsemane, at night, when, naturally, the sun was darkened. But in addition to this ordinary "darkening of the sun," all the Gospels report there was a great darkening over Jerusalem during the Crucifixion (presumably caused by a severe weather event).

Now, imagine the dispirited disciples after the Crucifixion. They'd been through a lot in the previous twenty hours or so. They'd been expecting their beloved Master to emerge as the Messiah in all his glory, via the dramatic events they believed must accompany the Day of the Lord.

But, instead of an initial, successful small battle, which they'd expected would initiate the whole chain of events, Jesus instead was humbly arrested, tried, and executed in a hideously gruesome fashion, on a day that became as physically dark as the event itself.

So they're going to wherever they will "celebrate" the Passover, though they're in absolutely no mood for it at all. They've been *defeated.*

And then the moon rises.

A *darkened, ugly-looking* full moon rises.

And the proverbial penny drops. Perhaps the ultimate *Aha!* moment in human history. The moment when the scales drop from the eyes, and suddenly, all that which was obscure and unclear, now suddenly becomes simple and obvious.

They'd already seen how the sun became darkened. But now, *the moon also was darkened!*

The prophecy was true! They *had* just lived through the Day of the Lord, though in a wholly unexpected way!

Jesus was still the Messiah after all!

This eclipse, then, is arguably the most important eclipse in human history. It gave the disciples reason to continue to hope and believe in their fallen Master. Without this

eclipse to bolster their confidence, Christianity itself may have become stillborn, and the whole subsequent history of the world unimaginably altered forever.

But wait? You still don't believe me?

In that case, consider the words of an actual eyewitness to the events in question, the apostle Peter, whose words on this subject have been recorded for posterity.

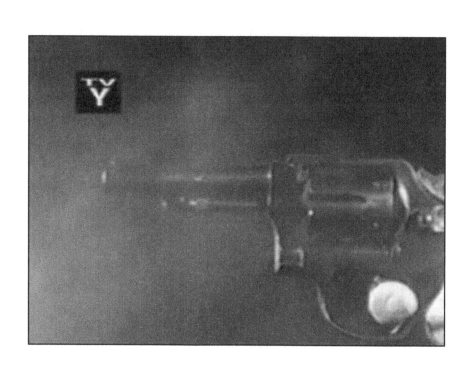

CHAPTER 9

THE SMOKING GUN

But Peter, standing up with the eleven, lifted up his voice, and said unto them, Ye men of Judaea, and all ye that dwell at Jerusalem, be this known unto you, and hearken to my words: for these are not drunken, as ye suppose, seeing it is but the third hour of the day. But this is that which was spoken by the prophet Joel; and it shall come to pass in the last days, saith God, I will pour out of my Spirit upon all flesh: and your sons and your daughters shall prophesy, and your young men shall see visions, and your old men shall dream dreams. And on my servants and on my handmaidens I will pour out in those days of my Spirit; and they shall prophesy: and I will shew wonders in heaven above, and signs in the earth beneath; blood, and fire, and vapour of smoke: the sun shall be turned into darkness and *the moon into blood*, before that great and notable day of the Lord come: and it shall come to pass, that whosoever shall call on the name of the Lord shall be saved.

(Acts 2:14-21, emphasis added)

The scene above is from Acts of the Apostles 2. It is some seven weeks after Passover, and the Crucifixion, and the disciples are gathered together to celebrate another Jewish pilgrim festival, called *Shavuot*, which we call Pentecost.[2] The text describes the descent of the Holy Spirit, and then the speaking in tongues to the multitudes.[3] Acts records that on this day, the first 3,000 persons were baptized and converted to Christianity.

Peter is telling the crowd several things: 1) The Day of the Lord has already come; 2) he, Peter, *personally* experienced the Day of the Lord; 3) he, Peter, personally saw the sun darken and the moon, not darken per se, but turn blood-red—*because that's what the moon does when under eclipse.*

Peter's discourse on the first Pentecost is the "smoking gun," the point that clinches the argument.

By seeing the sun darken (however that happened) and by seeing the moon turn blood-red (via eclipse), Peter himself is saying that the Day of the Lord, when Jesus became the manifested Messiah, happened several weeks earlier, and he *personally* witnessed it.

Summary and Conclusion

Since there were only two possible dates for the Crucifixion, and since the eclipse of April 3, AD 33, which made the moon turn blood-red, happened on only one of the two possible days of the Crucifixion, and since we have the apostle Peter's own words testifying to what he *personally* saw and witnessed, therefore there can be no doubt— *Jesus was crucified on April 3, AD 33.*

APPENDIX

A. Dr. John P. Pratt's letter to me of March 28, 2006

Dr. John P. Pratt
P.O. Box 752
Orem, UT 84059

March 28, 2006

James A. Nollett
163 Pond Street
Billerica, MA 01821

Dear James,

Thank you for sending me a copy of your booklet, "A Scientific Determination of the Exact Time and Date of the Death of Jesus of Nazareth." It is with pleasure that I respond to your request to review it and give my opinion of it. Although you explicitly state that you are not requesting an endorsement, I give you permission to quote this letter publicly if you so desire.

The booklet is well-researched and clearly explained. A compelling case is given that the crucifixion of Christ indeed occurred on Fri 3 Apr AD 33. Peter's quoting of Joel's prophecy that the moon would turn to blood does appear that he was trying to convince his audience that Christ was the Messiah because that prophecy was fulfilled right on the Crucifixion day. There is no doubt in my mind that Nollett's conclusion as to the time of Christ's crucifixion is correct.

A fellow researcher,

Dr. John P. Pratt,
Ph.D. (Astronomy)

P.S. Be sure to get the second edition of Jack Finegan's Handbook of Biblical Chronology which came out in 1998. The fact that you did not see that I had referenced the 1983 Humphries and Waddington paper in my 1985 paper on the subject allowed you to discover the lunar eclipse for yourself and be a second witness. My papers are all in printer-friendly format at www.johnpratt.com and are best found by using the search engine on the home page. The one contribution I feel I have made to this entire subject is that Passover not only prefigured the sacrifice of the true Lamb of God, but also his birth. My article on the subject is on my website, entitled, "Passover: Was it Symbolic of His Coming?" which I believe you would enjoy.

P.P.S. Also, I regret that it took so long for me to respond. Your letter was sent to my cousin, and after being forwarded to me, it was misplaced until last week.

B. Sir Dr. Colin J. Humphreys email to me of March 1, 2012

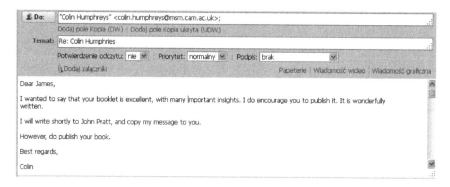

Dear James,

I wanted to say that your booklet is excellent, with many important insights. I do encourage you to publish it. It is wonderfully written.

I will write shortly to John Pratt, and copy my message to you.

However, do publish your book.

Best regards,

Colin

BIBLIOGRAPHY

1. Feldman, W. M. *Rabbinical Mathematics and Astronomy*. 3rd ed. England, Sepher-Herman Press, 1978.

2. Finegan, Jack. *Handbook of Biblical Chronology: Principles of Time Reckoning in the Ancient World and Problems of Chronology in the Bible*, rev. ed. Peabody, MA: Hendrickson Publishers Inc. 1998.

3. Humphreys, Sir Dr. Colin J. *The Mystery of the Last Supper: Reconstructing the Final Days of Jesus*. Cambridge: Cambridge University Press, 2011.

4. Langer, William L., comp., ed. *An Encyclopedia of WORLD HISTORY*. Boston: Houghton-Mifflin, Cambridge: Riverside Press, 1940, 1948.
   (William L. Langer was the Coolidge Professor of History at Harvard University.)

5. Nollet, James A. "Astronomical and Historical Evidence for Dating the Nativity in 2 BC." *Perspectives on Science and Christian Faith*, vol. 64, no. 4., 2012.
   (This article is available for public viewing from their website, www.asa3.org.)

6. Pratt, Dr. John P. "Yet Another Eclipse for Herod," *The Planetarian*, vol. 19, no. 4, Dec. 1990.
   (The paper is also available from Dr. Pratt's own website www. johnpratt.com.)

7. Ratzinger, Joseph (Pope Benedict XVI). *Jesus of Nazareth: The Infancy Narratives*. Whitmore, Philip J., tr. New York: Image, an imprint of the Crown Publishing Group, a division of Random House, Inc.

ENDNOTES

Foreword

1. My late father read my original booklet in his final years, as he was reposing his soul to meet his Maker, and told me it brought him great comfort in that it buttressed and reinforced his own lifelong staunch Roman Catholicism.
2. See in the Appendix a "snapshot" of Dr. Humphreys' actual full e-mail message to me.

Chapter 1 Notes

1. There is no such a thing, of course, as the "year 0." There is 1 BC ("Before Christ") which is immediately followed by AD 1 AD ("*Anno Domini*," which is Latin for "the Year of the Lord." In AD 525, a Christian monk named Dionysios Exiguus invented the current system of BC/AD. He calculated that Jesus was born about 754 AUC, which is a Latin acrostic which means "*ab urbem condita*," or "from the time of the establishment of the City (of Rome) by the mythological Romulus and Remus, and defined this year as year 1 of the new era.

2. Luke 3:23 says that Jesus was "about" thirty years old when he began his public ministry.

3. The Gospel of John says that Jesus spent the third and final Passover of his career in Jerusalem—though it also implies that he spent his first Passover there too, when he triumphantly entered Jerusalem, which suggests he may have been there twice. (Actually, John records still other visits, including one on Chanukah.) A theory of two visits also explains the great secrecy of the location of the Last Supper. More about that in due course.

Chapter 2

1. A. T. Olmstead, "The Chronology of Jesus' Life," *Anglican Theological Review*, XXIV (January 1942), 23-26.

2. Jerry Vardaman and Edwin M. Yamaguchi, editors; *Chronos, Kairos, Christos: Nativity and Chronological Studies Presented to Jack Finegan* (Winona Lake: Eisenbrauns 1989) 61–63; also personal letter of July 10, 1993 to Jack Finegan.

3. G. Ogg, "Chronology of the New Testament," *Peake's Commentary on the Bible*, edited by Matthew Black (London: 1962), p. 728; G. Ogg, "Chronology of the New Testament," *The New Bible Dictionary*, edited by J. D. Douglas (1962), p. 223.

4. *Contra Heraesii.*

5. *Stromata.*

6. *An Answer to the Jews*, c. 8.

7. *Homilies on Luke.*

8. *The History of the Church.*

9. *Panarion.*

10. *Seven Books of History Against the Pagans.*

11. Jack Finegan, *Handbook of Biblical Chronology*, § 519, Table 146, Page 302, who cites Schürer, *A History of the Jewish People in the Time of Jesus Christ*, 5 volumes (New York: Scribner's 1896); re-

vised edition G. Vermes & F. Millar, 3 volumes in 4 (Edinburgh: T. & T. Clark, 1973–1987) vol 1.1, 350–357; Pauly-Wissowa, *Real-Encyclopädie der klassischen Altertumswissenschaft (Real Encyclopedia of Classical Ancient Knowledge)*, Zweite Reihe (Second Row) 4.2, col. 1629.

12. *Antiquities, 18.1-2.*

13. *Ibid, 18.4.*

14. *Contra Marcion, 4.19.*

15. This disagrees with the generally accepted list of governors of Syria which, according to Finegan (see Note 9 above) ran like this: 9–6 BC, Saturninus; 6–4 BC, Publius Quinctilius Varus (the same who was killed, with three entire Roman legions, in the Teutobergerwald in Germany, in AD 9); 3 –2 BC, Quirinius, 1 BC–AD 4, Gaius Caesar (Augustus' grandson, through his daughter Julia and Marcus Agrippa). A different Saturninus (L. Volusius Saturninus) is listed for AD 4–5, then Quirinius again for AD 6–7.

Tertullian (See Note 12 above) said that Augustus took a census while Saturninus was governor of Syria, and while Varus was in Jerusalem, waiting to succeed Saturninus. Since it is known that Augustus ordered a census in the year 8 BC, that would satisfactorily account for the above chronology, save that the census of 8 BC counted only Roman citizens. Tertullian's reference has caused the creation of a secondary, alternative, hypothetical list of possible Roman governors at this time, listing Varus twice (2 BC the second term), who evidently and therefore succeeded Saturninus both times.

There has been a tablet found near Rome, on the grounds of what was Varus' estate, attesting to an unnamed man who was twice governor of Syria. The fact that it was found near Varus' residence strongly suggests Varus was the unnamed two-time governor.

The common-sense interpretation of Tertullian's word is that he believed the census of 8 BC to be the census involving the birth of Jesus as recorded by Luke, despite the fact that he named Saturninus and not Quirinius as the governor, which contradicts Luke's Gospel.

My conclusion is that Tertullian twice made an error, in the first place by ignoring Luke's account naming Quirinius, which he had to have known about, and secondly by misidentifying the census of the nativity as Augustus' enrollment of all Roman citizens in 8 BC, when in fact the census of 2 BC (See text above and Note 14) far better harmonizes with Luke's account. Jesus and his parents would not have been counted in 8 BC because they weren't Roman citizens, but since the census of 2 BC was for the purpose of making *all* the inhabitants of the Roman Empire swear an oath acknowledging Augustus as *Pater Patriae*, *everybody* would have been included in it.

16. *Antiquities 17.41 – 45.*

17. *Adv. Pag.*VI.22.7, VII.2.16, translated by R. J. Deferrari, *The Fathers of the Church* (Catholic University Press of Washington DC, 1964), Vol. 50, pp. 281, 287.

18. *An Encyclopedia of WORLD HISTORY*, compiled and edited by William L. Langer, the Coolidge Professor of History at Harvard University, p. 32, (published by the Houghton-Mifflin Company of Boston and the Riverside Press of Cambridge (Massachusetts), copyright 1940 and 1948.

19. Joseph Ratzinger a.k.a. Pope Benedict XVI, *Jesus of Nazareth/ The Infancy Narratives*, pp. 61–62, translated from the original German by Philip J. Whitmore, translation copyright © 2012 by Libereria Editrice Vaticana, published in the United States by Image, an imprint of the Crown Publishing Group, a division of Random House, Inc., New York.

20. Dr. John P. Pratt, *Yet Another Eclipse for Herod*, The Planetarian, Vol. 19, No. 4, Dec. 1990, pp. 8–14. The paper is also available

from Dr. Pratt's own website www.johnpratt.com. Speaking of which, all reading this note are warmly invited to spend some time visiting Dr. Pratt's website, for it is full of very interesting matter about calendars like the Mayan calendar, and how to time certain events from the Bible and other cultures.

21. Schürer, Emil, *The History of the Jewish People in the Age of Jesus Christ* (Edinburgh: T. & T. Clark, 1973), vol. 1, p. 257.f

22. Martin, *Star*, 174– 79, 232–234. He writes about the Lapis Tiburtinus, the stone (See Note 13) found near what was Publius Quinctilius Varus' estate outside Rome.

23. *Antiquities*, XVII.ii.1, XVII.v.2.

24. Flavius Josephus is the famous "turncoat," notorious in Jewish history. He initially was a leader of the Jewish revolt against Rome, which broke out in AD 66. He was captured, and instead of being executed (probably by crucifixion), he somehow convinced the Roman Generals Vespasianus and his son Titus of his value to their cause, serving thereafter as their advisor. He took on the name "Flavius" as a token of being in their clientage. He left behind a history of the Jews (*Antiquities*) and the *History of the Jewish War*.

25. *Antiquities* XIV.xvi.4 (year specified by the two consuls); XVII. vi.4, viii.1, xiii.2, XVIII.ii.1, iv.6; *A History of the Jewish War* II.vii.3.

It should be noted that a pair of men always served one calendar-year terms as consuls of Rome, and careful records were kept of who was consul in what year. For example, in the year 694 AUC, what we call 59 BC, the consuls for that year were Gaius Julius Caesar and Marcus Calpurnius Bibulus. Historians in later years might then refer to events of that year as having happened "during the consulships of Caesar and Bibulus." Matching some event with the time of the consulships of X and Y is therefore a very solid way of dating that event.

26. T. D. Barnes, *Journal of Theological Studies*, 19 (1968), 204-9.

27. Ernest Martin, *The Birth of Christ Recalculated* (Pasadena: FBR Publications, 1980).

28. *Antiquities 14.389 & 487, and 17.191*, and *The Jewish War, 1.665.*

29. Babylonian Talmud Tractate *Rosh HaShanah 10b.*

30. For astronomical information, I have used a program throughout this book called *Skylights*, written and copyrighted in 1994 by G. Vecchi, and sold by Zephyr Services of Pittsburgh, PA.

31. Unless otherwise stated, all times stated herein refer to Jerusalem local time, when the position of the sun at its zenith (when exactly half the day has ended) is defined as 12 o'clock high noon. Modern Jerusalem of course lies in a modern time zone. Since it lies somewhat to the east of the exact center of the time zone, local (astronomical) high noon occurs several minutes earlier than the nominal 12:00 which is the same throughout the time zone. This will involve a correction factor of some 8–25 minutes or so (depending upon the time of year). I will make all the corrections.

32. W. E. Filmer, "The Chronology of the Reign of Herod the Great," *Journal of Theological Studies* 17 (1966), 283– 98.

33. According to Robert Graves in his *I, Claudius*, which eventually was made into a hit PBS series, Gaius Caesar was poisoned by his evil stepmother Livia, Augustus' wife.

34. See comment at the beginning of this chapter, and Note 4.

35. *Antiquities XVII.ix.5; Dio Cassius lv.9-10.4*; Barnes p. 208.

36. Robert Graves, *I Claudius*, Vintage Books, p. 81.

37. Dio lv.10.4, from Cary, E., *Dio's Roman History* (Cambridge: Harvard University, 1980).

38. Finegan, *Ibid*, § 518.

39. Filmer, *Journal of Theological Studies* 17 (1966): 298; Barnes, *JTS* 19 (1968): 205; Riess, *Das Geburtsjahr Christi* (*The Year of Jesus' Birth*) (Freiburg: Herder, 1880); Beyer, "Josephus Re-examined."

40. Beyer, *Ibid*, 4.

41. Dionysios Exiguus was *correct* in assigning Jesus' birth to the year 1 BC. But assigning December 25 as the exact birthdate simply has no historical justification.

    In the first place, late December even in Judea is cold, clammy, and damp—as I personally well recall from my Christmas Eve visit to Bethlehem during the Gulf War (1990). (Due to the war, there were only a few dozen persons present that year; I almost had the whole city to myself!) Luke 2:8 says, "And there were in the same country shepherds abiding in the field, keeping watch over their flock by night." That's *hard* to do in December! So I highly doubt Jesus was born then.

    So why did Dionysios Exiguus pick December 25 as the specific birthdate of Jesus? It was in response to prevailing fashion, and as yet another example of Christianity's ability to absorb pagan traditions and then transmogrify them into Christian traditions.

    A few examples will suffice: a) The great Cathedral of Chartres sits on what was Cenabrum, the central site of Celtic-Druid worship, scholarship, and civilization. It was long considered to be a nexus of strong spirit-forces, so Christianity co-opted "The Force" (with apologies to the *Star Wars* franchise) by Christianizing it. b) The author Fr. Andrew Greeley once reported that in Ireland, there is a shrine to St. Bridget, but in the pagan times before the arrival of St. Patrick, it was the pagan shrine to the goddess Brigitte. Fr. Greeley reported, it was not only obvious, but also laudable, that Christianity had co-opted this pagan goddess and turned her into a Christian saint. And c) I myself have witnessed the power of Christian transmogrification. In the ten years that preceded my retirement and move to Poland, I lived in Boston, Massachusetts. Boston's North End is an Italian/Sicilian enclave, and has about ten private religious societies that the Catholic Church—to its *chagrin*—does *not* organize and direct. Among these are the St.

Anthony's Club, the Santa Lucia Club for women which shares its facility with the St. Anthony's Club, the Sant' Agrippina Club, the San Giuseppe Club, the Fishermen's Club, the Madonna della Cava Club, etc.

Really, these clubs are hangouts, where members go to smoke, drink, play cards, watch football games, stay away from their wives, gamble, and *perhaps* on blessedly *rare* occasion violate club rules and commit such naughty deeds as selling drugs or exchanging stolen goods or whatever. (But I never saw a thing—not a *thing*, I tell you!)

But somewhere inside every club, however profanely its members may otherwise behave, somewhere maybe in a corner or on a separate floor, is a shrine to the saint in question. Do not be deceived, for all the non-religious activities that go on inside the clubs, the members' devotion to the particular saint and shrine is *devout and genuine.*

And every summer, each of the clubs has a weekend reserved for it when the members take the statue of the saint in question and mount it on a litter and carry it through the streets, exactly as they used to transport the Roman emperor or some other powerful Roman bigshots. Each saint visits all the other saints in their clubs so they can all catch up on the past year's gossip. And each saint drops by all the Italian businesses, and the businesses donate money to the saint, which is pinned to the saints with ribbons, and the saint grows fatter and fatter with money by the minute, and this goes on all day long. (God help the clubs if the United States Treasury ever gets smart and stops printing $1 bills and replaces them with dollar coins; the clubs could go out of business!)

I played trombone for years in an Italian street band whose job it was to follow the saint(s) and play Italian melodies anytime anybody donated money. Yes, summertime in Boston's

North End is festival time, and everybody has a simply grand time. "When the Saints Come Marching In," indeed!

So why do I mention all of this? It's because these Italian Christian religious clubs actually have very ancient and *pagan* roots. Ancient pagan Rome had many deities that it imported from places such as Greece and Egypt. But peculiar to the real, native Latin religious spirit was their sense and belief in *numina*, which were non-corporeal, faceless, nameless spirits or forces, which were the spirit "bosses" of a particular street intersection or a stream or something like that. The *Lares* and *Penates* were considered household and family godlets and godlings, each specific to a particular house of family. The movie *Gladiator* portrayed this very well, with the Russell Crowe gladiator character retaining little figurines which represented his beloved wife and son, which his African friend eventually buried in the sand of the arena at the end of the movie after the gladiator died.

In Rome and throughout Italy, major street intersections were liable to have something called a "crossroads college." These too were hangouts: members could come in and drink, eat, exchange stolen goods, procure the services of a prostitute, etc. But in these clubs, there was always a corner reserved for whatever nameless godling or spirit who happened to be the boss of that particular turf and jurisdiction.

My Italian clubs in Boston are simply the transmogrified and Christianized, latter-day versions of these old crossroads colleges. Such is the power and success of Christianity to co-opt and absorb whatever pagan traditions it encounters.

So why do I mention all of this? It goes back to why Dionysios Exiguus picked December 25 as the birthdate of Jesus Christ.

Exiguus didn't invent the idea of December 25 = Christmas, not at all. Celebration of December 25 as the birthdate of the Christian Savior is something that had been going on for centuries, by the time of the sixth century. He just sort of made it official in his designation of BC and AD.

So why then did the early Christians celebrate Christmas on December 25? The reason is simple: December 25 had already been the centuries-long and established Roman tradition of the *Saturnalia*. The Saturnalia was a week-long festival timed to coincide with the winter solstice. It culminated on January 1 at a ceremony held at the temple of the literally two-faced god Janus (hence the name of the month), who had a face for looking ahead and for looking back, which is what we all do on New Year's Day.

(When Julius Caesar reformed the Roman calendar, he made it a point to commence the Saturnalia on the day of the winter solstice. In other words, in the time of Caesar, the solstice of winter fell not on December 21 or 22, but on December 25. As any anthropologist would attest, many cultures throughout history have celebrated midwinter day, the day when the days are the shortest and the sun is the lowest it can be in the sky, because after midwinter day, the sun is destined to climb into the sky again and bring a return to warm, long, sunny days. Making the day of the winter solstice fall on the Roman Saturnalia was simply Caesar's own way of making sure Rome would always celebrate the return of the sun.)

As another sign of the Church's ability to co-opt and transmogrify older festivals, the Church not only co-opted Christmas Day but also January 1 too, which originally was its own festive day in Rome, when not only was there a ceremony at the Temple of Janus, but was also the day on which the new consuls for that year were sworn in at the Temple of Jupiter *Optimus et Maximus* (Jupiter Best and Greatest).

So what did the Catholic Church call *this* day, which happened to be New Year's Day? Well, here's a hint: Counting inclusively, New Year's Day is exactly the *eighth* day following

Christmas Day = 1ˢᵗ day of the Saturnalia (= winter solstice day).

Does that remind anybody of something from the Old Testament?

Well, here's the answer: For centuries, and until some time after the Vatican II Council, the Catholic Church co-opted/transmogrified/Christianized Janus/Roman New Year's Day *by calling it the Feast of the Circumcision of Jesus.* Because, in Judaism, circumcision of male babies occurs on the eighth day after their birth, so it was a handy coincidence the Church could use to convert both the first day of the Saturnalia and its final day, the Roman New Year's Day, both into Christian days.

The holy Feast of the Circumcision was one of the half-dozen solemn Holy Days of Obligation of the Catholic church-year. And it still is—save that the Church stopped calling it "the Feast of the Circumcision of Jesus" a couple of decades or so ago.

Which was just as well, for evidently the same sense of irony finally occurred to the Catholic powers-that-be that also occurred to Yours Truly, too many years ago, when both I and the world were young(er). *Why on earth* was the Catholic Church commemorating *the day when Jesus became a Jew, a member of the covenant of Moses, literally a* b'nai Brit, *a "son of the (old) covenant"?* Since the whole purpose of Jesus coming to earth was to institute a *new* covenant to replace the *old* covenant?

I don't know what the Catholic Church calls this Holy Day of Obligation these days, but whatever it is, it's no longer "The Feast of the Circumcision."

I will close these notes, and this chapter, by telling a little-known fact.

We know that when Julius Caesar reformed the Roman calendar, he intentionally intercalated, or added, sixty-seven days after the end of December in a one-time-only "month" called "Intercalis," in order to make the seasons of the year agree with the calendar seasons (46 BC was about 421 days long by Caesarian decree: 365 + 67–11 (to account for the slightly shorter twelve-lunar months year). Caesar intentionally added the right number of days necessary to make the winter solstice fall exactly on December 25, the first day of the Saturnalia.

Given this, then why does today's winter solstice fall some three or four days *before* Christmas?

Julius Caesar defined the length of the year as exactly 365.25 days long, and by adding an extra day every four years, our customary "leap year," this allowed his civil calendar to keep up with the astronomical or climatological year.

However, the actual earthly year is slightly shorter than Caesar's defined length. The actual length of the astronomical year is some 365 days, 5 hours, 48 minutes, and 46 seconds. This means that the earth's seasons every year run some 11 minutes and 14 seconds faster than Caesar's civil year, with its year defined as exactly 365.25 days long. That means every 128 years or so, the earth's seasons have gained an entire day on the civil calendar.

Now come to the year 1582. It is just after the Council of Trent, during which the Catholic Church strived for some twenty years to rid itself of its vices which had helped bring on the Protestant Reformation (or, "Protestant Revolt" if one were Catholic!), and one final thing that Pope Gregory XIII believed he needed to reform was the civil calendar, to bring it in line once again with the seasons of the year – because by 1582, the winter solstice was falling, not on December 25, but around December 12, because the seasons had gained some 13 days on the civil calendar.

So Pope Gregory brought back the seasons with the calendar year by decreeing that October 5–14 of 1582 did not, never did, and never would exist. So 1582 was a year of 355 days, in which October 4 was followed, not by October 5, but instead by *October 15.*

But here the perhaps careful reader may ask, but if the calendar had fallen *thirteen (13)* days behind the seasons, why then did Pope Gregory only remove *ten (10)* days from the calendar? Did Pope Gregory make some kind of computational error?

And the answer is *no*, he did not. Pope Gregory quite purposefully and intentionally cut out fewer days than necessary to bring the calendar back to where it was in the time of Julius Caesar.

And his reason was quite simple. Given his one-time opportunity to do what very few men have ever done—reform an entire calendar—he wanted to make as meaningful as he possibly could. In his religious, Catholic world, that meant honoring Catholic Christianity in some fashion.

The Council of Nicea was held in the year AD 325, and was arguably the most important Church council of all time, because it resolved many lingering questions of doctrine and organization which had plagued the Church since its inception, and which could never before be addressed due to the underground, persecuted nature of the Church.

To honor the work of that Council, Pope Gregory deliberately and intentionally cut out only enough days from the civil calendar to make it line up with the way the seasons agreed with the civil calendar in the year AD 325, and in that year, the winter solstice fell on December 22.

And *that* is why in our modern, Gregorian reformed calendar, the winter solstice will never fall on Christmas Day, as it did for Julius Caesar, but instead, for now and forever, will always fall on December 22.

Chapter 3

1. Image of the gold aureus of the Roman Emperor Tiberius is taken from an image of a coin present in the British Museum.
2. Sir Dr. Colin J. Humphreys, *The Mystery of the Last Supper* (Cambridge University Press), p. 20.
3. In Greek, "tetra" means "four." A "tetra-arch," or a "tetrarch," is the ruler of a quarter of something. But there were three surviving sons, so why weren't they "triarchs" or something like that? The answer is, after their father died, the three surviving sons were given a cut of the territories he'd ruled. His kingdom was cut into quarters. Herod Archelaus received two of the quarters; and each of the other sons got one-quarter.
4. According to John 18:13, Caiaphas was in fact the high priest; Annas was his father-in-law. Matthew 26:57 also confirms that Caiaphas was the high priest.
5. All New Testament quotes, unless otherwise stated, are from the King James (Authorized) Version (KJV).
6. *Suetonius*, ed. J. C. Rolfe, (LCL) vol. 1, 323.
7. Humphreys, *Ibid*, Page 19.
8. Tacitus, *Annals 15:44*.
9. Josephus, *Antiquities 18:89*.
10. Professor White actually believed Jesus could have been crucified as early as AD 27. But given his own belief that the career of John the Baptist began no earlier than late in AD 26, it is impossible to see how this could be.
11. *Mesechta Shabbat ix.3*, Talmud Yerushalmi.

Chapter 4

1. Most people believe—certainly Jews—that this has *always* been the case. However, in his book, already cited, Dr. Humphreys contends, at considerable length, too, that until the time of the Babylonian captivity (about 600 years before the time of

Christ), Judaism observed calendar days which began at *sunrise*, and during that captivity adopted the Babylonian custom of commencing their days at sun*down*.

It is certainly true that the present names of the twelve months in Judaism are of Babylonian origin. Indeed, the name of at least one Jewish month, Tammuz, also is the name of one of the pagan gods of the Babylonian pantheon. Given Judaism's insistence on the absolute unity of God and the non-existence of all other gods; given that Judaism *loathes* all strange gods, it is startling that Judaism allows the name of a pagan, false god to grace one of its months, but there it is.

This book need not concern itself with the virtues of the morning-based calendar of the Jews prior to the Babylonian Exile, since its sole purpose is to discover the date of the Crucifixion, which occurred after the Jews returned from Babylon and indisputably used the same evening-based calendar they continue to use today. Whatever calendar the Jews may have used centuries before the Crucifixion is therefore of little relevance to the subject of this book.

However, I will say one brief thing in defense of Dr. Humphreys' theory of a pre-exilic calendar.

At the time I wrote these words, I was also the author of a monthly column in *The Jewish Press*, in which I offer my translation of a book originally written and published in German in 1935. The name of the book is *Die Juden in der Welt*, or, *The Jews in the World*, and is a country-by-country survey of the history and the times of Jews in all the countries of the world, such as countries existed in 1935 (no Korea at all, and a united Czechoslovakia, for example).

The original author was Mark Wischnitzer. He opened his chapter about the Jews of Cyprus by tracing the origins of that community to the Persian King Cyrus, and followed to the point of its rebellion against the Romans at the time of the Emperor

Trajan, who "gave the Jewish resistance bloody persecution, expulsion, and extermination" so that there were no more Jews left on Cyprus.

Or so Trajan thought. Evidently, he missed isolated Jews way deep in mountains of that island, for Wischnitzer then wrote, "Benjamin of Tudela, in his travel throughout the world in the latter part of the 12th Century, found Jewish communities on Cyprus. He became acquainted there with a sect of Jews there who, oddly enough, celebrated the Sabbath from early on the Sabbath until early on Sunday." In other words, their Sabbath day began at sunrise, Saturday morning, and lasted until Sunday morning.

I passed this information along to Dr. Humphreys, who expressed to me his belief that this isolated clan of Jews continued with the old pre-exilic calendar because they were cut-off from the rest of the Jewish people, too isolated to have received the word that the rest of the Jewish people had switched to a sunset-based calendar. Such things happen, as we know in our times with our recent discoveries of still-existing stone-age cultures in places like New Guinea and the Amazon rainforest.

Mark Wischnitzer, *Die Juden in der Welt*, (Berlin: The Erich Reiss Verlag) 1935, p. 76.

My translation appeared in *The Jewish Press* of Brooklyn, NY, on September 27, 2011.

2. Unless otherwise noted, all translations from the five books of Moses are from *The Pentateuch and Rashi's Commentary*, by the Rabbis Abraham ben Isaiah and Benjamin Sharpman, in collaboration with Dr. Harry M. Orlinsky and Rabbi Dr. Morris Charner (Philadelphia: S. S. & R Publishing Company, Inc., 1949, the press of the Jewish Publication Society.

3. A "synodical month" is the time from one new moon to the next. It is about 29½ days long. It's another way of saying the amount of time the moon needs to form a next conjunction

with the sun. It is also about two days longer than an actual astronomical, or "sidereal" month, which may be defined either as the period of a complete lunar revolution around the earth, or the amount of time needed for the moon to return to a given point in the zodiac where it was a month before. The reason for the gross difference between the two months is due to the fact that while the moon orbits the earth, the earth orbits the sun, so in the time the moon has completed one revolution around the earth, the sun in the meanwhile has advanced through about 1/12th of its own course through the zodiac, and the moon needs a couple of days more to catch up.

4. It is pronounced with a hard "s," as in "Nissan." Since that's the Roman-letter spelling of the name of a certain Japanese automobile maker, it's probably advisable to spell the name of the Jewish month of *Nisan* with a single "s"!

5. Professor Anthony Saldarini of Boston College was also kind enough to review and critique an earlier version of this book for me. He said, ". . . 'dusk' is based on an ambiguous Hebrew expression "between the settings". . . a rabbinic text (later) says that the Hebrew expression refers to the time when the sun begins to descend, i.e., from midday on."

The "rabbinic test" he may have had in mind is the following Rashi commentary on Exodus 12:6: "From six hours [after noon] and upward, it is called 'bain ha-arivim,' when the sun declines toward the place of its setting to become darkened. And the expression 'bain ha-arivim' appears in my sight to refer to those hours between 'the evening of the day' and 'the evening of the night.' The 'evening' of the day is the 7th hour, from the time that 'the shadows of evening are stretched out' (Jer. 7:6); and the 'evening' of night is at the beginning of the night. Erev denotes evening and darkness, as in Isaiah 24:11, 'All joy is darkened ('erevah')."

("Rashi" is short for "RAbbi SHlomo ben Yitzhcak," who was a prolific Bible and Talmud commentator who lived in France in the eleventh century. He is perhaps the most beloved of all the Jewish Bible and Talmud commentators.)

Leviticus 23:5 uses the word *aravim* to refer to "dusk." It appears this word can mean an after-sundown darkening, or any time after the sun passes its zenith in the middle of the day.

The Jewish evening prayer service known as *ma'ariv* might be helpful here. It is generally recited about forty minutes after sundown or later, so it is surely quite dark by the time it's recited. The first sentence of *ma'ariv* ends with the expression, ". . . *asher b'diboro ma'ariv AREVIM,"* or, "by Whose [God's] Word creates the evening from dusk." The context is clear—*arevim*, or dusk, brings in *ma'ariv*. Both words are cognate with the word *erev* which, as we've seen from the Book of Genesis, means evening or night-time.

Furthermore, the word *bain* which Rashi uses means "between," the separation of one unit of time from another, ". . . *bain yom u'bain leilah,"* "separating between day and night," is another passage from the evening prayer service.

The *Kittzur Shulchan Aruch* ("The Abbreviated Table of [Jewish] Law") says concerning the forthcoming Passover meal, "Although on every other Sabbath and festival it is permissible to recite the Kiddush and have the meal while it is yet daylight, so as to add from the secular to the sacred, on Passover it is not permitted to do so, because the precept of eating matzah on Pesach is to be performed only at night, as was the case with the paschal sacrifice, about which it is written (Exodus 12:8), 'And they shall eat the meat on this night.'"

Combining Exodus 12:8 with Leviticus 23:5-6, it is clear that it is at dusk, on the fourteenth day of the month, as that day is *ending* and giving way to the fifteenth day at dusk, is when Passover starts. Prof. Saldarini's comment *might* be tenable for any other holiday of Judaism save Passover, but is not tenable concerning Passover itself.

6. Professor Saldarini was of the opinion that the meaning of this passage has been controversial since ancient times, since it could mean either that the sheaf (of barley) was offered on the day after Passover, or on the first Sunday after the first Sabbath after Passover—in other words, on the first Sunday after Passover, regardless of which day of the week Passover fell upon. In the event Passover itself fell on a Sabbath, the difference would be moot.

What does the expression "day of rest" mean in this passage? The Hebrew text itself uses the single word "*Shabbat*." Normally, this word refers to Saturday, the seventh day of the week, since the very word *Shabbat*" is cognate with the word for the number seven, *sh'va*. If that's what *Shabbat* means in this passage, then Prof. Saldarini is correct.

However, that runs counter to the Rashi commentary on this very passage that says, while the verse does indeed use the word *Shabbat*, in reality, "festival" is meant.

There are indeed Hebrew words for "festival"—*hag* and *moed* come immediately to mind. However, it is not wrong to refer to all of these as "*shabbat*," since festivals too are days of rest. In fact, there are only small differences in the laws governing behavior on festivals and sabbaths.

Furthermore, there is the matter of *Sefirot ha-Omer*. This is the countdown—actually, the count-up—to the wheat harvest. In synagogues to this day, beginning on the second night of Passover, a count-up to the wheat harvest is commenced. Forty-nine days are counted; then the next day is *Shavuot*, or the Festival of Weeks.

Keeping in mind that the Jewish liturgy, its cycle of daily, weekly, and seasonal prayers, was designed to mimic the sacrifices in the temple as a verbal analogue, if Prof. Saldarini were correct, then the Jews would always commence the count-up to the wheat harvest on the Sunday after Passover, and *Shavuot* would therefore always fall on a Sunday. But this is never the case. The counting of the *Omer always* commences on the evening of the second night of Passover, wherever in the week it may happen to fall.

However, Prof. Saldarini possibly may be correct in one instance. Though Passover today may never fall on a Thursday night, due to the automatic nature of the present Jewish calendar, in ancient times, when months commenced on any day of the week, in some years the second night of Passover, which was the same as the first night of the counting of the *Omer*, could fall on *Shabbat*. In this case, the counting *might* have been put off until the following evening. Such a thing happens with *Teines Esther*, the Fast of Esther, which normally falls on the day before Purim, but is pushed back a day when Purim falls on a Sunday, because it is forbidden to fast on the Sabbath.

I doubt this is the case. But if it is, then it creates all the more reason to suppose that Shavuot fell on a Saturday night—Sunday in the year of the Crucifixion—in other words, the first Pentecost.

7. *Chulin 60b.*

8. *Rabbinical Mathematics and Astronomy*, by W. M. Feldman. It was originally written, in England I think, around 1928–1931. I have the "Third, corrected edition," copyright 1978, by Sepher-Hermon Press.

Feldman cites this Maimonides writing: *Hilchoth Kiddush Hachadeshim* that literally means, "The Laws of the Holy New Moons."

"This however is only the case if the moon's true longitude lies between 270 degrees (1st of Capricorn) and 90 degrees (1st of Cancer.]) For [lunar] longitudes between 90 degrees and

270 degrees (Cancer to Capricorn), the corresponding true elongations limits are 10 degrees and 24 degrees respectively.

What did Feldman mean above when he spoke of Capricorn and Cancer?

The moon takes a west-to-east track through the zodiac. It crosses into Capricorn, then two weeks later, on the other side of the zodiac into Cancer, having in the meanwhile entered the autumn and winter zodiacal signs of the likes of Aquarius, Pisces, Taurus, Gemini. Then, after transiting through Cancer, the moon tracks through spring and summer signs like Leo, Virgo, Scorpio, Sagittarius, etc. (as do the sun and the planets in their own ways).

Feldman is saying that Maimonides said, when the new moon can be found in zodiacal signs such as Pisces, Aquarius, Taurus etc, while transiting from Capricorn toward Cancer, the Maimonides' 9 degrees–15 degrees rule applies; but when the new moon can be found in such signs as Leo, Virgo, Scorpio etc," then the limits are 10 degrees–24 degrees.

The new moon of Nisan when Jesus lived could be found more or less in Pisces, which is right in the middle of the range. For our considerations, Maimonides' 9 degrees–15 degrees rule *definitely* applies.

I'm not certain if this makes any modern astronomical sense, but it ought not make any difference in any event.

It is true that Maimonides operated under the Ptolemaic Epicycle theory, which a few centuries later was disproven by Johannes Kepler. (Maimonides wrote his work around 1178.) But he, and his fellow rabbis for the previous 1000+ years, knew to within a few seconds the duration of a *mean* synodical month. (Due to perturbations in the moon's orbit, and the earth's about the sun, and due to elliptical orbits, actual synodical months can occur several hours earlier or later than the mean length of a synodical month—but the rabbis could account for these things.) As long as the Ptolemaic system worked, in an empirical sense, it made no difference whether it were a correct model of the universe.

Count on it – Maimonides had all the technical, *accurate* data he needed to write what he did.

And it really doesn't even matter. Because, even if Maimonides were inaccurate, the plain historical fact is, he reported on the behavior of the calendar council of Jerusalem as they functioned in the days of the temple. They behaved, for better or for worse, however correctly or incorrectly, as Maimonides described.

So when we try to go back in time and determine whether a new moon were visible in Jerusalem or not, we scientific historians need to understand how the people thought and behaved at the time, and tailor our modern findings in the light of their understanding.

Chapter 5 Notes

1. "And you shall have [it, the Paschal lamb] in keeping until the fourteenth day of this same month (of Aviv, or Nisan) and there shall slaughter it. The whole assembly of the congregation of Israel [shall slaughter the lamb] at dusk" (Ex. 12:6). In other words, at the end of the fourteenth day of the month (sunset), as the fourteenth day is becoming the fifteenth day, is the time to slaughter the lamb, for this is the beginning of the day of the festival.

2. There is a sheer logistical present here. Given the throngs of pilgrims which used to crowd into Jerusalem in these times, tens if not hundreds of thousands of lambs had to be slaughtered within very brief time. Humphreys (*ibid.*) noted that Flavius Josephus wrote that the slaughtering commenced at around 3 P.M. Given the Rashi commentary on Exodus 12:6, already cited

in Note 5 in the previous chapter, defining "evening" as being any time after the middle of the day at high noon, this would give the lamb-slaughterers enough time to get their job done.

3. *Kitzur Shulchan Aruch, Abbreviated Code of Jewish Law 113:2*, "A compilation of Jewish Laws and Customs," by Rabbi Solomon Ganzfried, translated by Hyman E. Goldin, LL.B. This is the "Annotated Revised Edition" by the Hebrew Publishing Company of New York, copyright 1961 and 1963. Of knowledge and belief, Rabbi Ganzfried prepared this version from Rabbi Joseph Caro's original version.

 But do see Dr. Humphreys' book! To reiterate, his book contains an amazing theory that Jesus was *not* using the same calendar that the overwhelming majority of Judean Jews were using. Jesus was Galilean, not from Judea, and Dr. Humphreys argues that in Galilee, at least some of the Jews were using a slightly different calendar, dating from the days before the Babylonian exile. While this book does not directly concern itself with such arguments, and therefore won't go into them, Dr. Humphreys' book, *The Mystery of the Last Supper,* is highly recommended.

4. *Mishna Sanhedrin 4:1.*

5. Prof. Saldarini objected to my use of the word "Sanhedrin" in this context. He said, Jesus was not tried before the full Sanhedrin, but rather before some politically powerful members of the "Jerusalem council."

 It is true that the Gospel of John mentions no full trial, but rather only a personal interrogation by the high priest. Presumably, the *Kohen Gadol* would not have been alone; he'd have had subordinates present while he interrogated Jesus, so perhaps this could be the "Jerusalem council."

 However, Matthew 26:59 says, "Now the chief priests, and elders, and all the council, sought false witness against Jesus, to put him to death." The parallel passage in Mark says the same thing. Luke refers to the "elders of the people (the Pharisees), the high priest, and the scribes (Sadducees, though some believe the word "scribe" = "Pharisee"). Putting these together is tantamount to saying "Sanhedrin."

Given the scriptural absurdities of holding a trial on the festival itself, Prof. Saldarini therefore may well have a point; the full Sanhedrin did not try Jesus on the night of the festival because it *could* not try him, not legally, anyway. So therefore, perhaps a more *ad hoc*, less legal, and smaller rump body, such as a "Jerusalem council," tried Jesus.

Chapter 6 Notes

1. March 23, AD 30 fell on a Thursday. But, how do I *know* this?

    I *could* derive this fact by calculating such dates by hand. But I could *easily* make an error. I need therefore a sure-fire method that affords me the luxury of certainty.

    My astronomy program Skylights does not calculate dates directly. But it does furnish something called "Julian days" which enables one to calculate all dates of human history, quickly and readily.

    What are "Julian days"? Despite the name, they have nothing to do with Julius Caesar. "Julian" in this context refers to a nineteenth century French mathematician of that name.

    He believed the earth was created precisely on January 2, 4713 BC. Furthermore, he defined the precise time as 12:00 high noon, Greenwich mean time! I used to wonder why he didn't define his day one as commencing at midnight GMT, but it occurred to me that he probably chose 12:00 high noon GMT in order to harmonize with the newly-created international date line, so that at the stroke of midnight on the IDL, not only would all civil days be the same, but so too would his "Julian days."

Anyway, he called January 2, 4713 BC (and why not January 1? I don't know) day one. The next day, January 3, 4713 BC, he called day two, and so forth up to our present time. Every next succeeding day therefore has been assigned its own specific and unique Julian number.

For example, Election Day in America, November 3 1998, corresponded to Julian day 2.451,121, which means that exactly 2,451,121 days lapsed between January 2, 4713 BC and November 3, 1998.

Julian days are useful in this manner: When one divides any Julian day by 7, the remainder (if any) can be used to determine which day of the week it was. Consider the example of Election Day '98. All Americans know that elections always fall on Tuesdays. The Julian number for November 3, 1998 is 2,451,121. When divided by 7, this number yields a remainder of 1.

This means, any Julian number throughout history that yields a remainder of 1 after being divided by 7 *must* be a Tuesday! The same logic holds for any other Julian number that yields any other kind of remainder.

Consider the following three examples:

October 12, 14 hundred and 92, "when Columbus sailed the ocean blue," and discovered "India." The Julian number for this day is 2,266,296 which, when divided by 7, yields a remainder of 4. Since days with no remainder are Mondays, and days with a remainder of 1 are Tuesdays, that means Columbus discovered America on *Friday*, October 12, 1492.

Then there's July 4, 1776. The Julian number for this day is 2,369,916. This number, when divided by 7, yields a remainder of 3. That means the Declaration of Independence was signed on *Thursday*, July 4, 1776.

And finally, consider Sunday, December 7, 1941, the day of the Japanese attack on Pearl Harbor. Most Americans know that this "day which shall live in infamy" was the first Sunday in December of that year, and was picked by the Japanese for the Pearl Harbor attack for precisely that reason. The Julian number for this day is 2,430,336. When divided by 7, this number—predictably enough—yields a remainder of 6, which is the remainder that corresponds to Sundays.

To summarize the rule: When Julian Numbers are divided by 7, the Julian number in question either was evenly divisible by 7, or yields a remainder. The remainders correspond to each of the days of the week as per this table:

Sundays correspond to Julian remainders of 6.
Mondays correspond to Julian remainders of 0.
Tuesdays correspond to Julian remainders of 1.
Wednesdays correspond to Julian remainders of 2.
Thursdays correspond to Julian remainders of 3.
Fridays correspond to Julian remainders of 4.
Saturdays correspond to Julian remainders of 5.

A reader at this point, however, who's astute enough to know the history of the evolution of the modern calendar, and who knows about the Gregorian reform, might well object at this point: Does my program take the Gregorian reform into account?

See Note 41 of Chapter 2 for the short history lesson of how Julius Caesar reformed the Roman calendar, and the minor error in his calendar. As stated there, Pope Gregory XIII instituted two reforms. His first reform was to catch up the solar year with the civil year by decreeing that *ten* days, October 5–14, 1582, *never existed* as a matter of official papal fiat.

Now, Pope Gregory's fiat was recognized at the time only by those countries that accepted his authority, and at this time in history that excluded the Protestant and Eastern Orthodox countries that wanted nothing to do with any "papist" decrees, and who only gradually, over the course of the next several centuries, recognized this reform.

England, for example, only adopted Pope Gregory's reform in 1752. When it did, it changed the birthdates of all living Englishmen so that, for example, George Washington, who originally was born on February 11, 1732, had his official birth date change to February 22. This annoyed Englishmen to no end!

In the case of Russia, the Tzarist government never accepted Pope Gregory's reform, and that is why the Communists long celebrated Red *October*, even though they celebrated Revolution Day as *November* 7, because, in the calendar that was used by the Tzarist government, Revolution Day fell in *October*. Russia only adopted Pope Gregory's reform after the modern Communist state was established and imposed.

The Eastern Orthodox religions haven't accepted the Gregorian reform to this day, which is why Orthodox and Catholic Easters usually don't coincide. According to Dr. Humphreys, there's an island off Scotland that also hasn't adopted the Gregorian Reform to this day.

Pope Gregory's second reform was to adjust how to calculate leap year. Here is the minor reform he instituted: a) Every four years, as always, there will be a leap year, save b) in years which end with "00," such as 1800, 1900, 2000, etc. c) In such years, leap year will *not* occur if the two digits ahead of the "00" are numbers that are not evenly divisible by 4, which is the case with 18(00) and 19(00). d) When the first two digits of a given year ending in "00" are evenly divisible by 4, which was recently the case with the year 2000, then this year will have its leap year as usual.

In this manner, three times every 400 years, there will be no leap year, and this will enable the civil calendar to keep pace with the true, astronomical, solar year.

In closing, the reader may be *certain*, that if I state such and such a date fell on a Wednesday, then, in fact, it did.

In all the calculations in this book, the *assumption* will be that all dates after October 15, 1582, are Gregorian reformed dates, and all dates prior to October 4, 1582 are according to the old calendar of Julius Caesar. It will also be assumed that all Roman governments following Julius Caesar faithfully and rigidly conducted its business with his calendar. This may not in fact have always been the case in the early days, but as long as we understand this as an assumption and definition, it really makes no difference.

For example, some people reading my past edition of this book have criticized the exact date I selected as the date of the Crucifixion. In such cases, it usually transpires that they have calculated the date of the Crucifixion by assuming, as a matter of definition, that the Gregorian reformed calendar was in effect during this time, which it wasn't. But, in this case too, the discrepancy is harmless as long as it's understood and defined, for it is the Julian number that is truly significant.

2. "Jerusalem local mean standard time" means that the program determines when sunrise and sunset were on any given day. The program itself expresses these time as GMT+2. However, I have made note of when sunrise and sunset occur. From this, it's easy to calculate the number of minutes in a given day. Midday, when the sun is at its zenith, is defined as occurring when exactly half of the length of a given day has lapsed. Since Jerusalem lies several degrees to the east of the nominal center of its modern "time zone," that means that local high noon falls several minutes before 12:00, as defined by my program. I, however, am defining midday as 12 o'clock local high noon, which requires me to adjust the times my program gives me. My times are not mean, but instead are local, with an equal

amount of day falling before and after local high noon. This is what I call "Jerusalem local standard time."

3. Right ascension is a form of celestial longitude. Just as on earth longitude and latitude can be used to identify any location, so too can this system be used in the heavens, if we imagine we're at the center of a sphere, and the sky is the inside surface of a great ball surrounding us—which in fact was the ancient belief.

    Right ascension can be expressed either in degrees, or in units of time, where 1 hour = 15 degrees of a circle. By knowing the right ascensions of both the sun and the new moon, one can determine the closely approximate degree of separation between the two since, at any given time, both lie at the almost identical level of celestial latitude. Since 1 hour = 15 degrees, 36 minutes worth of difference = 9 degrees of arc separation.

    Celestial latitude is known as "declension." All stars have fixed declension and right ascension values, just as all places on earth have fixed latitudes and longitudes.

4. As previously stated in Notes, Sir Dr. Colin J. Humphreys has recently written a very ingenious book, *The Mystery of the Last Supper*, in which he reconciles the apparent contradiction between the Synoptic Gospels and the Gospel of John by showing why it's at least arguably plausible that the Last Supper was indeed a celebration of Passover, but that it occurred on *Wednesday* and *not* Thursday evening, with Jesus celebrating the Passover "two days earlier" than the masses of Jews in Jerusalem because he was operating on an older version of the Jewish monthly calendar in which days commenced at sunrise, not sunset, and in which months commenced after the last sighting of the *old* moon.

    I don't pursue this issue any further in this book for two reasons: 1) Dr. Humphreys' book speaks very well for itself and needs no corroboration from Yours Truly; 2) Unlike Dr. Humphreys, I am solely concerned with proving the date of the

Crucifixion, and the issue of which calendar Jesus may have used isn't particularly germane to that end.

However, Dr. Humphreys' book is *indispensable* for those who have further interest in the su

Chapter 7

1. There is a lengthy prayer for the Jewish High Holidays (*Rosh HaShanah* through *Yom Kippur*) called *Avinu Malkeinu* ("Our Father, Our King"), which consist of several dozen short declarative sentences about God, all of which begin with "*Avinu Malkeinu.*" The very first of these statements is, "*Avinu Malkeinu, ain lanu Melech eli Ata*"—that is to say, "Our Father, Our King, we have no King but You." There is a famous and hauntingly beautiful melody used in synagogues at this time, based on the final of the *Avinu Malkeinu* statements, and called "*Avinu Malkeinu,*" which has been recorded by many artists such as Barbra Streisand and Luciano Pavarotti.

   Anyway, the first statement, "We have no King but You," reflects a tension that the Bible talks about which occurred among the Children of Israel after the death of Moses to the time of the rise of King Saul. For several centuries, the Children of Israel weren't ruled by any king, since only God could be their King, and instead were ruled by the judges. But then it came to pass that the Children of Israel clamored for a king since they wished to be like the other nations. Speaking through the Prophet Samuel, God reluctantly agreed to give them a king if they desired one, but added that they might not like it in the end.

   Which reflects the wisdom of the old Irish saying, "Be careful of what you wish for—because you just might get it."

2. A modern Christian reading these words—doing so through the insulation and fog of 2,000 years of intervening history

and time—might well object at the characterization of Simon as a violent revolutionary, since it clashes with his sentiment that, since Jesus was the Prince of Peace, his disciples had to be peaceful too.

Such a Christian cannot deny Luke's calling Simon a "Zealot," but might be apt to defend it by remarking that this Simon was simply *extremely zealous* in his devotion toward Jesus.

This view is simply untenable. Recall when all the Gospels were written—during or after the First Jewish Revolt of AD 66–73. The Zealots at this time were as notorious throughout the entire Roman Empire, as the instigators of the revolt and as assassins, as Al Qaeda is today in the United States. When Luke named Simon as a "Zealot," his meaning would have been unmistakable to anybody in the first century reading his words. His Simon, one of the twelve highest disciples of Jesus was (if I may mix my metaphors) a Jewish jihadist.

3. According to STRATFOR, *sicario* is a current word used in Mexico to refer to killers employed by drug cartels. That this word also means a "hired killer" in Sicily and in southern Italy, I have on the good authority of my *paisan* Salvatore Pugliesi, the lead trumpeter for many years with the Roma Band of Boston, with whom I played for about ten years.

4. A case can be made, from evidence furnished by the Gospels themselves, that Judas Iscariot did *not* betray Jesus, though admittedly that is the obvious, plain reading of the Gospels.

First of all, what kind of "betrayal" can it be when the object of the "betrayal" knows perfectly well what is happening? All the Gospels portray Jesus as *knowing*, not only that he will be "betrayed," but knowing who will do it too. The Gospel of John reports Jesus as telling Judas, "Go, do what thou must."

It reminds me of an event which happened in Philadelphia, PA in the 1980s. There was an inner city/urban movement that was called, well, "MOVE." It was a strange fusion of back-to-nature squalor, People For the Ethical Treatment of Animals (PETA), Marxism, and African-Americanism.

They'd occupied a vacant house via squatting, and made pests of themselves throughout the neighborhood. They also literally *created* more pests, in that they lived in such unsanitary conditions that rats and mice thrived, and spread throughout the neighborhood. They broadcast music and political agit-propaganda at all hours of the day and night, and at all decibels. They didn't believe in garbage disposal, but did believe in saving animals, which was why their house was the primary source of the neighborhood's plague of filth and rats.

The neighbors begged the city to do *something* about MOVE. And the city did. They solved the problem forever, though not quite the way the neighbors had imagined or desired.

The city chased MOVE out of the house (killing many of its members in the process), by dropping an incendiary bomb through the roof. It not only burned MOVE's house to the ground; the resulting holocaust also burned seventy-three surrounding houses to the ground throughout the entire neighborhood, this being a neighborhood of old, dilapidated, fire-trap rowhouses.

Anyway, before the raid, MOVE was well aware that the city might make, well, a "move" on MOVE. Here are the verbatim words of Ramona Africa, minister of communications for the MOVE organization, speaking on behalf of its coordinator, John Africa:

"If you think y'all gone come in here and surprise us you are wrong. Thanks to the strategy of John Africa we are prepared for anything. We know that y'all would like us to think that long as the block aint evacuated we aint got to worry about no raid so that y'all can catch us off guard. M. aint never off guard! We know you people will try to raid this house by commin thru the walls on either side of the house and catch us off guard by allowing the people on the block to go about their business like nothin aint happenin.

"We know about the plastic explosives y'all can use to knock down walls to attempt to raid us swiftly and cleanly before any of the neighbors can get hurt. This is a—pipedream. The rain will not be swift and it will not be clean. The strategy of John Africa prepared us for anything y'all come up with, we will not be caught by surprise. To quote John Africa, the Coordinator, quote, *surprises only work when you succeed in surprisin somebody*, end quote—long live the Coordinator!"

Yes, indeedy. Surprises indeed only work when they succeed in surprising their intended target. Ramona Africa had it exactly right. And in the same way, surprise betrayals only work when the object of betrayal doesn't suspect the betrayal.

But Jesus not only suspected; he *knew exactly* what Judas was doing. If, after Judas departed to tip off the temple authorities, Jesus had a change of heart and decided he didn't want to accost/be accosted by, the temple authorities. If he had wanted to defy the Father and skip out on the entire save-the-world-by-being-crucified plan, all Jesus had to do *was not show up on the Mount of Olives*, to where Judas led the temple authorities, expecting to find Jesus.

Not only is it *obvious* that Jesus actually sent Judas to tip off the temple authorities, it's also *obvious*, when one thinks about it, that Jesus *had to have sent Judas* to inform the temple authorities where to find him.

Jesus *wanted and sought* the confrontation with the temple authorities—and moreover, he wanted it to occur specifically on the Mount of Olives. Otherwise, why not calmly wait for Judas to bring the temple authorities to the very building where they'd held the Last Supper?

If one is a traditional Christian, it is *obvious* that this *must* be so, because Jesus knew that he came to earth to be crucified and to atone for the sins of the world, and he couldn't do any of that unless and until he were first arrested. No arrest = no Crucifixion = no universal salvation for thee and thou. Since this was the whole point of Jesus' earthly ministry, it is therefore *obvious* that Jesus needed Judas, or someone like Judas, to act, *not* as his betrayer, but rather as his *messenger*, letting the authorities know where to find Jesus. Without having been tipped off by the likes of Judas, the authorities would not and could not have known to go to the Mount of Olives to arrest Jesus.

Furthermore—and at the risk of giving away the conclusion of this book—Jesus (also) may have had a very different purpose in mind. As we will see shortly, there were certain Messianic prophecies which Jesus was consciously trying to fulfill, and one of those prophecies holds the key to *proving* the precise day of the Crucifixion. It all has to do with the Mount of Olives, and being there armed with two swords . . .

But, getting back to Judas. I hold that he did nothing more than what Jesus required of him. As such, he was acting, not as Jesus' betrayer, but rather as Jesus' *faithful servant*, acting as he did to play his role in ushering in the kingdom of the Messiah, but a kingdom that would conform to what he and most Jews expected—an *earthly* kingdom.

When Jesus confronted the temple authorities, Judas, as the self-respecting Zealot and righteous killer that he was, fully expected Jesus to *win*. But instead, when the fiasco ended almost as soon as it commenced, not with victory but with Jesus' humble arrest, Judas *knew* that it could only end on a cross. In great despair because he'd *unwittingly* played this role in his beloved master's undoing, he hanged himself. When one sees Judas' actions in this light, his anguish is extremely psychologically compelling, and *authentic*.

And in this way, once the idea of Judas as a craven betrayer is stripped away, the account of this matter given by Matthew has a poignant and powerful ring of truth to it.

Judas has gotten a bad rap for all time.

5. By the way, kudos to Jesus' advance team. How was it that Jesus, on one fine day, did decide to hop onto a donkey's back, ride into Jerusalem and happen be greeted by thousands of overjoyed supporters? If you or I had done that in the first century, nobody would have given us a second glance. How was it that Jesus could do it and be greeted by throngs of ecstatic supporters? Was it spontaneous magic? Was it an accident or a coincidence? Did it happen by itself? Or did Jesus' advance team go into the city beforehand to spread the (good) word? I vote for the latter.

6. The apostles in particular, and the Jews in general, have always gotten a bad rap for having a lowly view of what the Messiah was supposed to do.

We look at their vision of the Messiah—an earthly, militant Messiah, bent on fomenting a literal holy war in order to achieve his purposes—as a vulgar, picayune, petty thing, grossly inferior to the actual majesty of the function of the Messiah, as Jesus (supposedly) saw it, and as hundreds of millions of Christians see it to this day. "My kingdom is not of this world." In other words, Jesus' kingdom was heavenly, and infinitely superior to the restricted, limited, unimaginative notion of the Messiah as everybody else understood the Messiah to be.

But actually, the first century Judean notion of the place of the Messiah was also, in its own way, very spiritual and lofty. For consider what it was they all expected.

They expected a redeeming Messiah who would drive out the hated Romans, and who would, in the words already cited of Zachariah, then go on to conquer the entire world, from sea to sea, but would speak peace unto the heathens, and would bring in a world without war or oppression, a world which, in the words of Isaiah, "the lion shall lie down with the lamb; the nations shall beat their swords into plowshares, and nations will no longer know war."

It would be a world in which the entire world would come to understand and serve only the One True God. It would be God's kingdom on earth.

In fact, the Christian view of the way the world will be after Jesus' Second Coming is pretty much the vision the Jews have always had of what the Messiah is supposed to accomplish— even the worldly, fighting would-be messiahs such as Shimon bar Kochba.

This is no vulgar, petty, profane thing at all. In its own way, this too is a highly lofty and spiritual vision. So, were the first century Jews *really* so far wrong?

7. This may seem far-fetched. Latin is indisputably an Indo-European language, which means its speakers descended, not from Shem, son of Noah, as did the Jews, the Arabs, and the Edomites, but rather from Yaphet, Shem's brother. Latins were doubtless part of the waves of peoples together with Farsis, Aryans, Greeks, Keltics, Germans, Slavs, and others, all of whom originated in the Caucasus Mountains where Mt. Ararat is, the mountain on which Noah's ark settled, and all of whom branched out from the Caucasus Mountains over the course of about 3,000 years to fill all of Europe, much of Asia, and later eventually spread to Australia and the Western Hemisphere. Our common *Caucasian* origins are why, if you are white and are arrested in the United States, the police indicate your race as *Caucasian*.

Furthermore, to believe the Roman legends, the founder of Rome was Aeneas, a Greek, not an Edomite.

However, there may well be much more than a grain of truth in the old Jewish legends.

The city of Rome was established in or around 753 BC. Before that, the *Etruscans* lived in what is now central Italy. The migrating Latins encountered the Etruscans in the area around Rome in the ninth and eight centuries BC, before displacing them via conquest.

Not a *lot* is known about the Etruscans. We do know that the early Latins absorbed their ways, and at least to a partial extent became Etruscan themselves.

And we know that the Etruscans originated from Phoenecia, which is more or less today's Lebanon. In other words, the Etruscans were, like the Carthaginians who settled at around this time in North Africa, *Semitic*. Like the Jews. Like the *Edomites*.

And so there lies the possible truth of the Jewish legends about Rome = Edom. Esau, Jacob's twin brother, has a far more malignant reputation in the Jewish midrashic literature than is readily apparent from the written Bible account. So, to equate Esau = Rome, is to make a very strong statement of loathing of Rome.

Chapter 8

1. The convention of 12-hour days (as opposed to 10-hour days, or 8-hour days), together with 60 minutes to the hour, is a concept the world borrowed from the Babylonians.
2. In a lunar eclipse, when, to an observer on the moon, the earth comes between the lunar observer and the sun, the "penumbra" is the portion of the earth's shadow under which some, but not all of the sun, is covered. When only a small portion of the sun is covered, it's not even noticeable on earth. As the percentage of solar surface covered increases, the darkening of the moon

becomes more and more noticeable. But there is never any clear line where it's totally light on one side and suddenly totally dark on the other. It is exactly the same with you and your shadow, where the edge of your shadow is blurry and indistinct, not sharp and clearly defined.

3. This is the portion of the earth's shadow on the moon under which the sun is completely covered. The portion (or entirely) of the moon under the umbral shadow of total eclipse appears either dark on earth, or, in the cases when much or all the surface of the moon is covered, the moon may frequently appear to be blood-red. This is due to the refraction, or bending, of the sun's light as it passes through the earth's atmosphere.

4. In my experience, this isn't enough shadow to cause a redness on the face of the moon. To an observer in Jerusalem, in addition to the 15 percent of hard umbral shadow, perhaps up to about 40 percent of the surface of the moon at this moment could have been observed to be under a blurry, smudgy kind of eclipse.

Chapter 9

1. This smoking gun image was taken from the Internet, and is a frame from the 57-second introduction to the 1950s *Superman* television series. Anyone who's seen these episodes knows how the lines go: "*Faster than a speeding bullet . . . more powerful than a locomotive . . . able to leap tall buildings in a single bound . . .*"

2. As already stated, Pentecost is the Christian word for the major Jewish pilgrim festival known as *Shavuot*, which literally means "sevens," representing a week of weeks (seven weeks) from Passover. It is regarded as the anniversary of *matan torah*, or the giving of the Torah (including the Ten Commandments) at Mt. Sinai. As still-observant Jews, the apostles had every reason to come together at this time.

3. A pet peeve of mine has long been pentecostalist/evangelistic services on television, watching either the minister himself, or his congregation, or both, ecstatically "speaking in tongues," and hearing so much nonsensical babbling coming from their mouths. It is totally out of the context of Acts 2, in which Luke the Evangelist makes it perfectly plain that the apostles were *not* babbling some kind of drunken gibberish, but instead were speaking intelligibly in their own ordinary language—presumably Aramaic—with the *miracle* being, anybody in the audience could nevertheless understand what the apostles were saying, in whatever language they best understood, regardless of whether they themselves knew Aramaic. Which, when you think about it, is a *far more* impressive miracle than the pseudo, non-miraculous noise of modern babbling "speaking in tongues."

CONTACT INFORMATION

To order additional copies of this book, please visit
www.redemption-press.com.
Also available on Amazon.com and BarnesandNoble.com
Or by calling toll free 1-844-2REDEEM.

Lightning Source UK Ltd.
Milton Keynes UK
UKOW06f2352260815

257580UK00002B/116/P

9 781632 326089